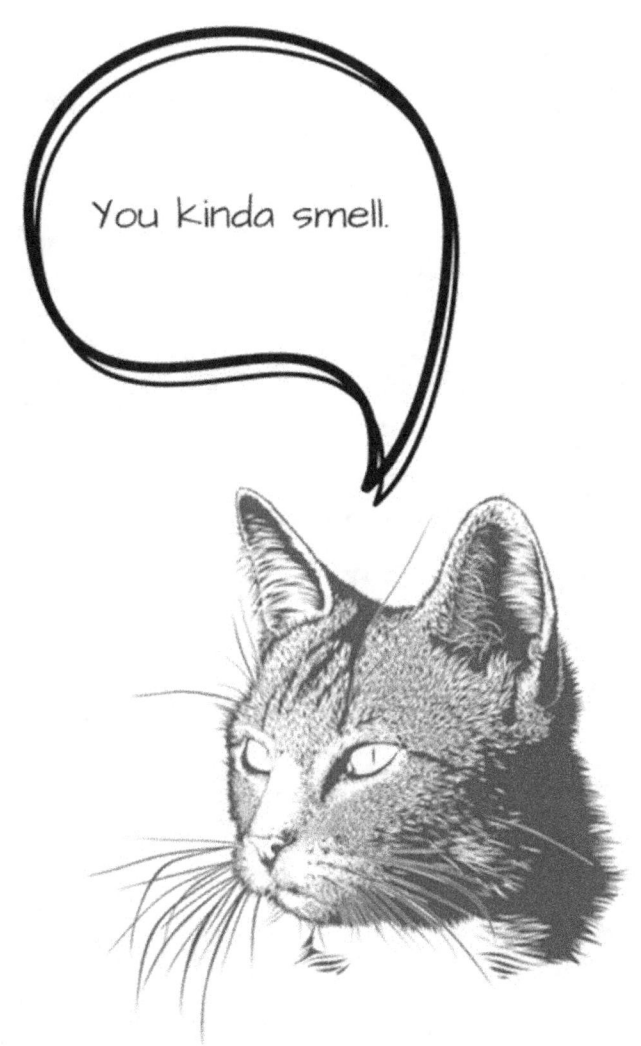

You kinda smell.

Animals Being Petty Coloring Book

By Mar y Sol

Is Pettiness your second language?

If the answer to that question is yes, then the Animals Being Petty Coloring Book is fucking perfect for you!

Whitin this book you will find 65 images to color, but be careful!! These animals are not playing any games. The savageness in these pages are no joke and the animals... well they don't care about your feelings.

The only rule for this coloring book?! Use as many colors as you want!

Mar y Sol

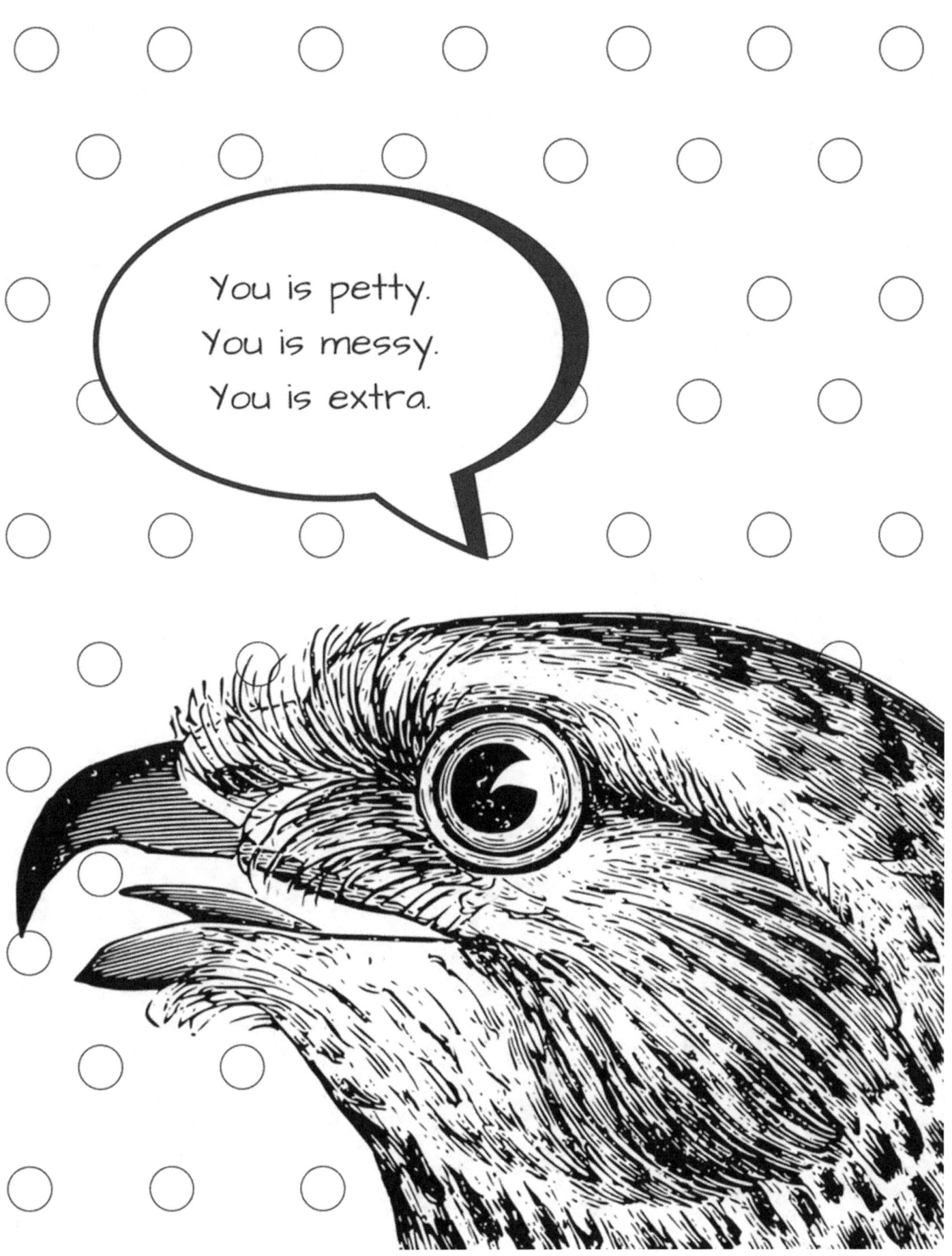

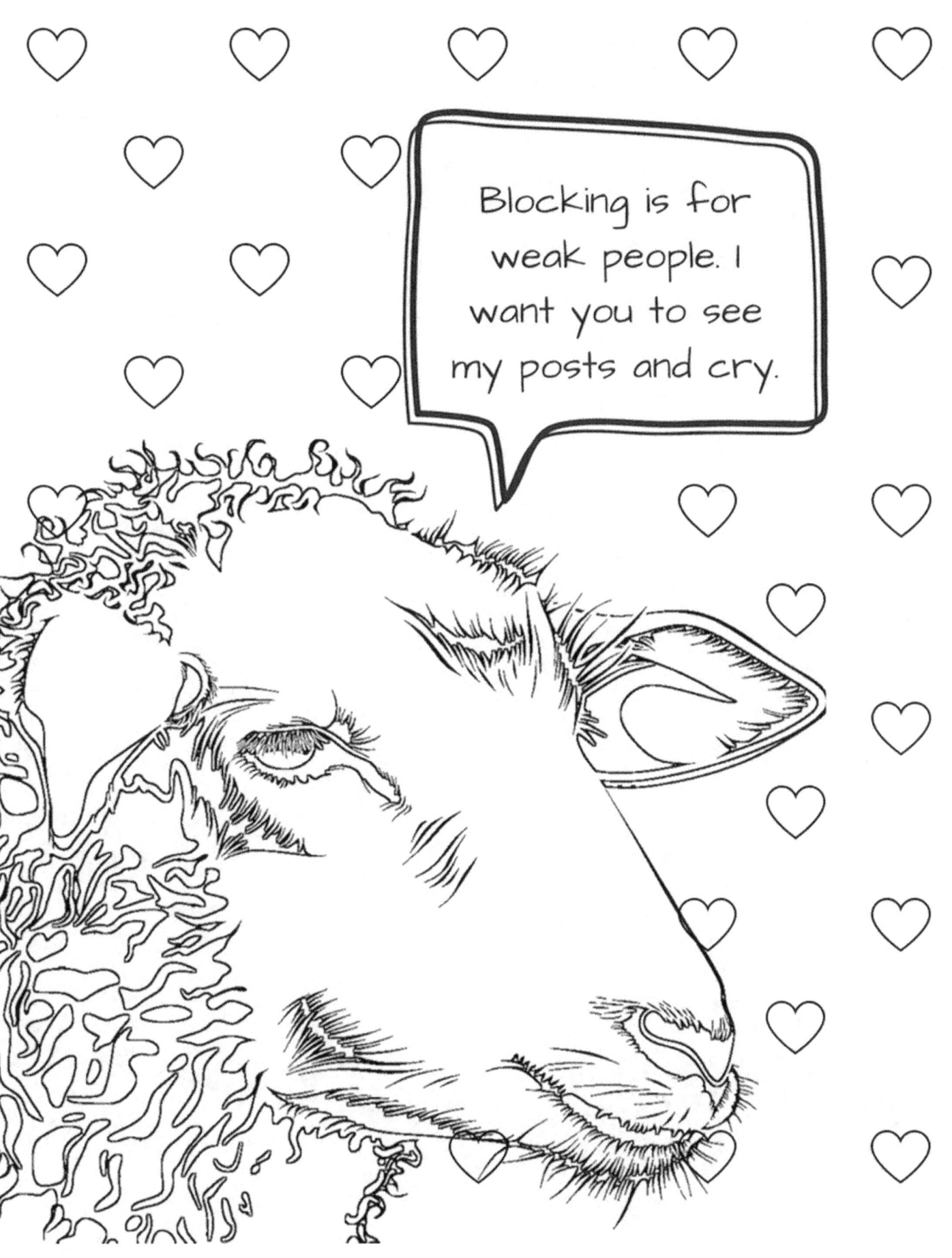

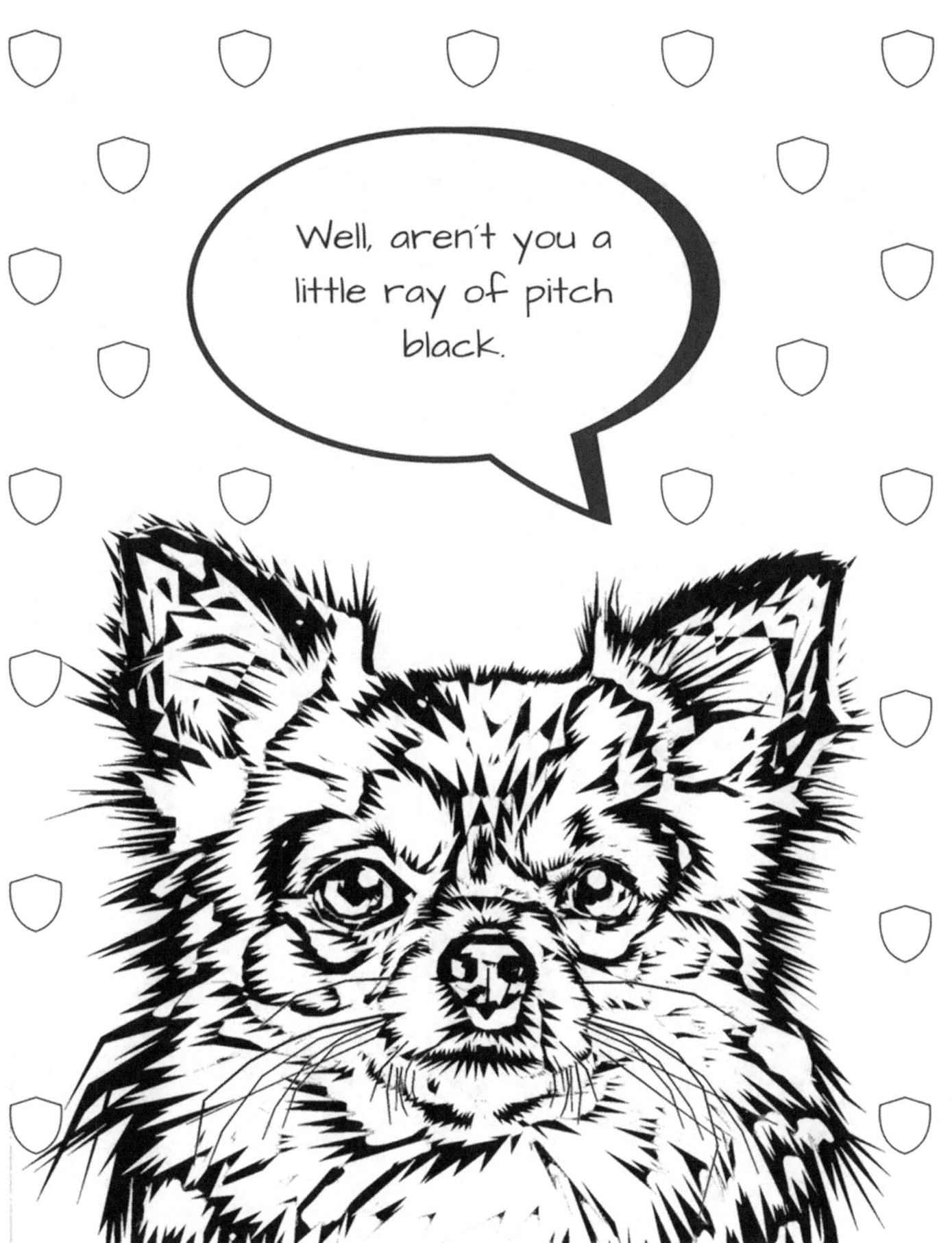

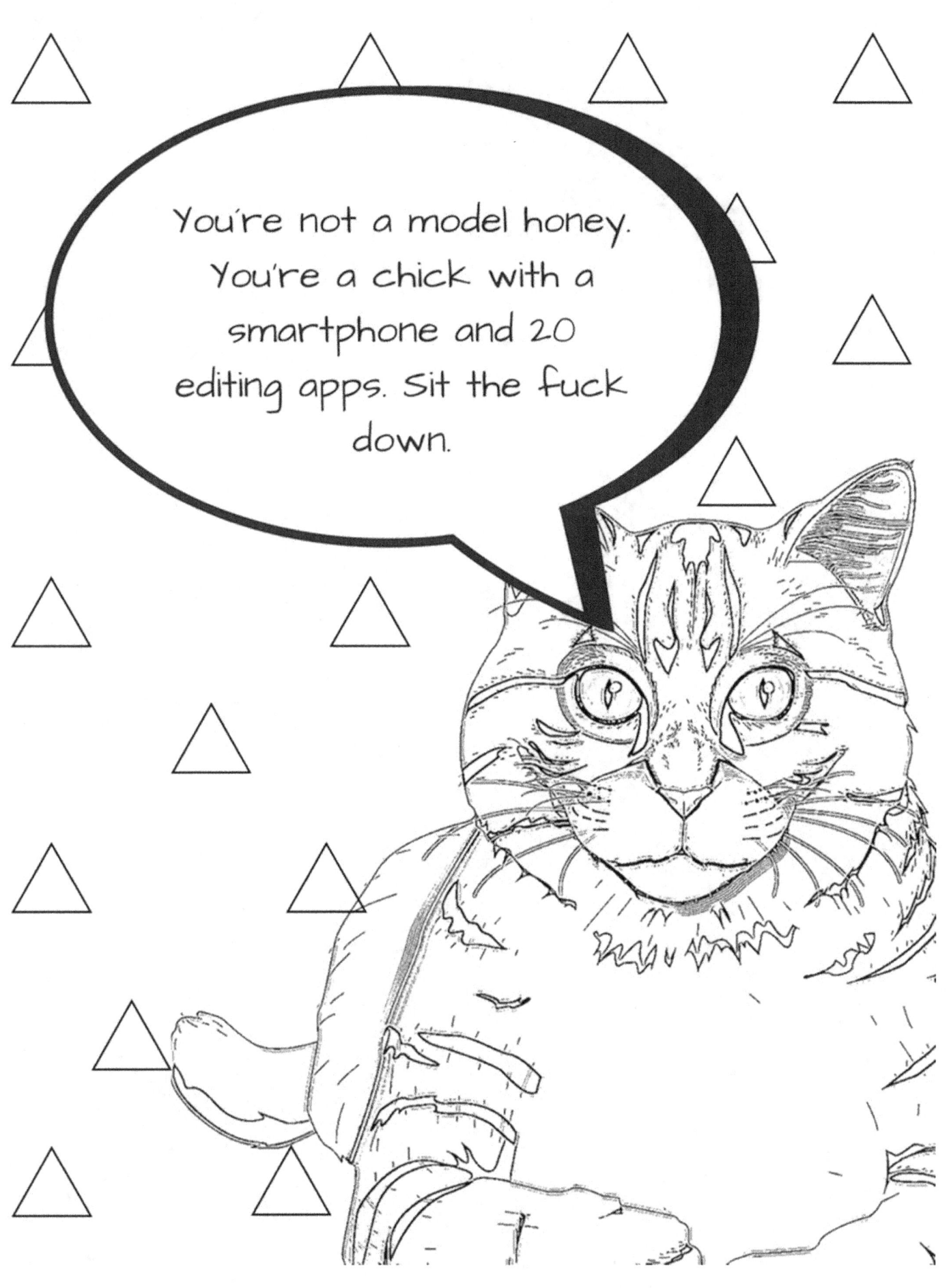

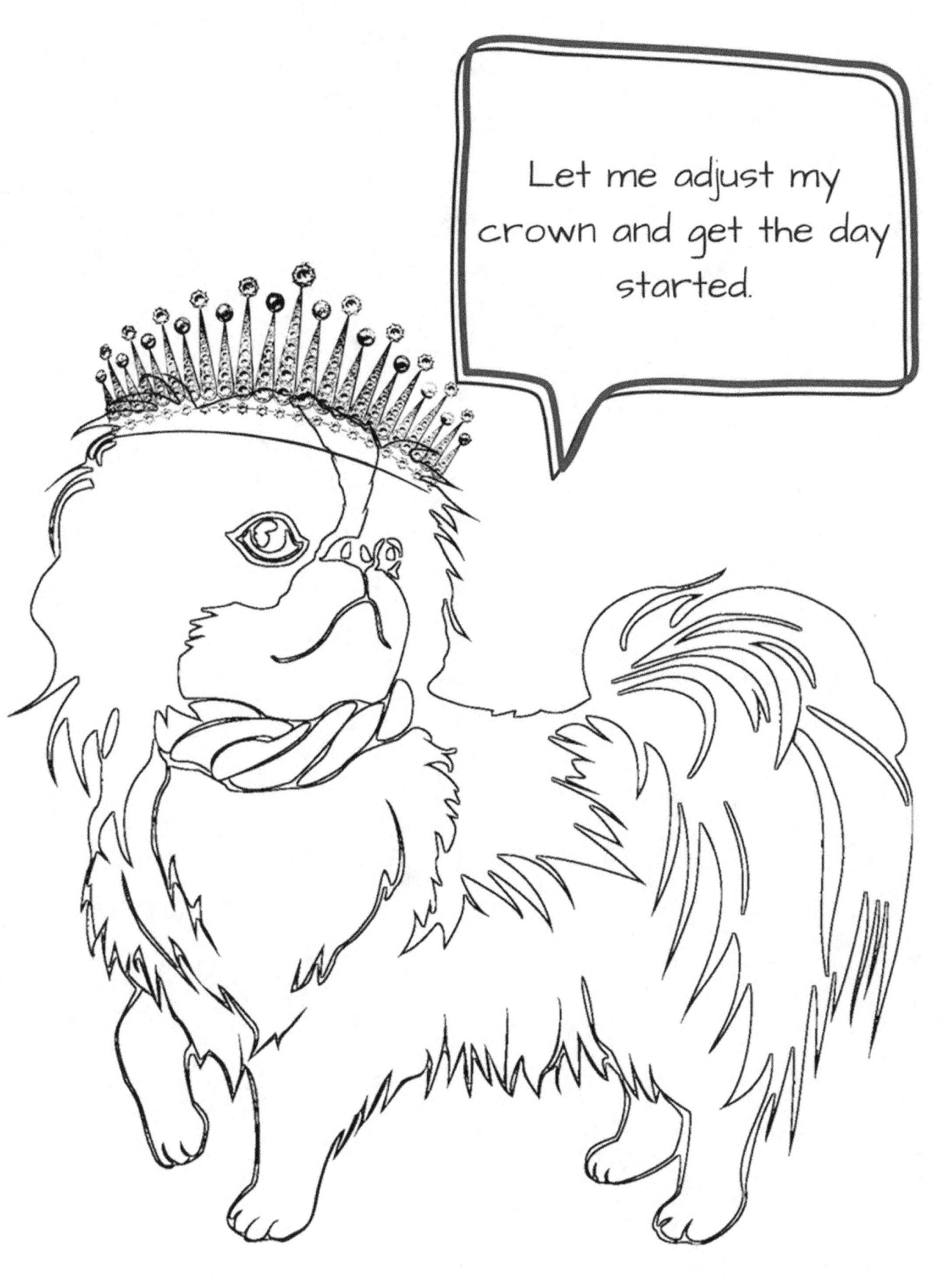

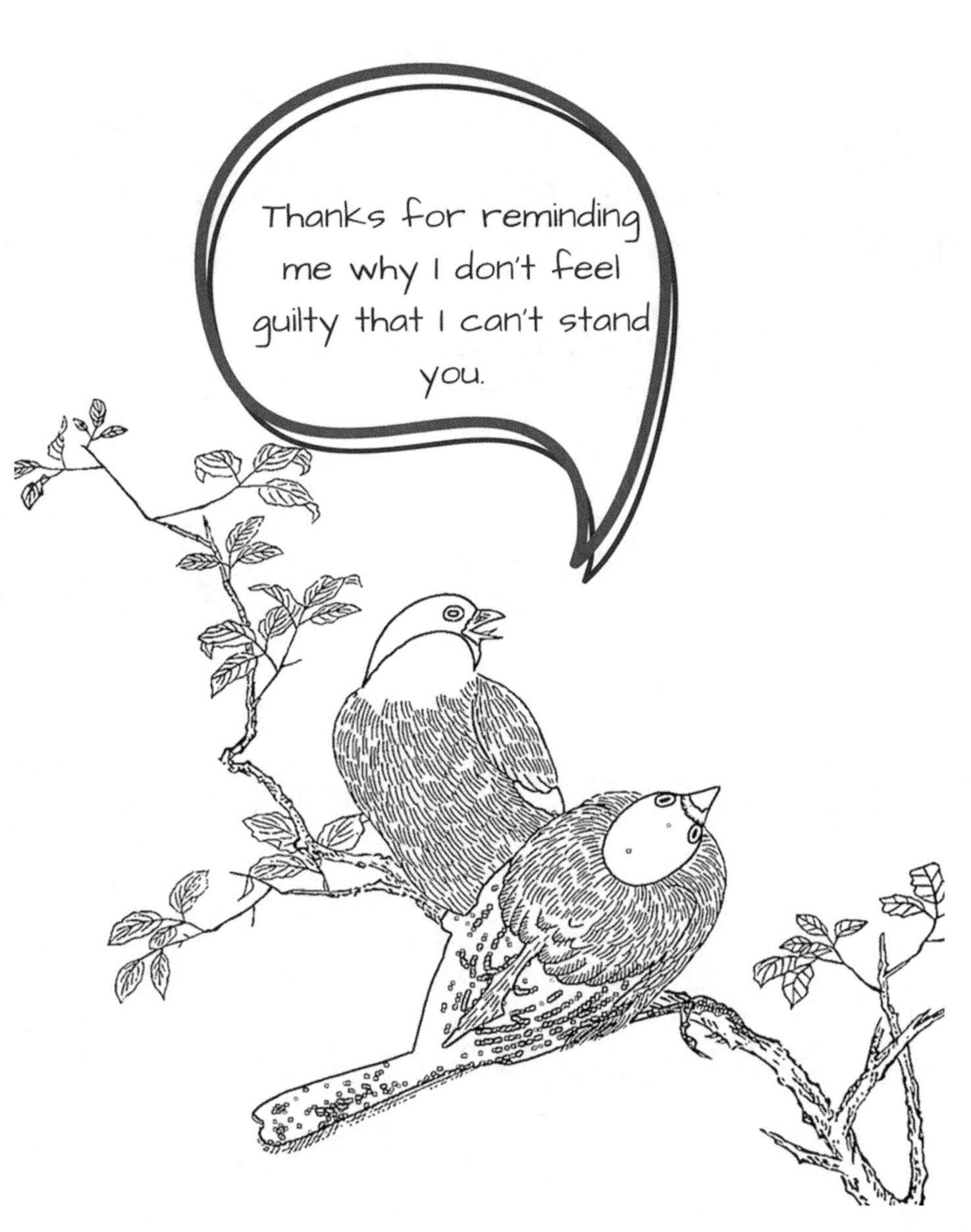

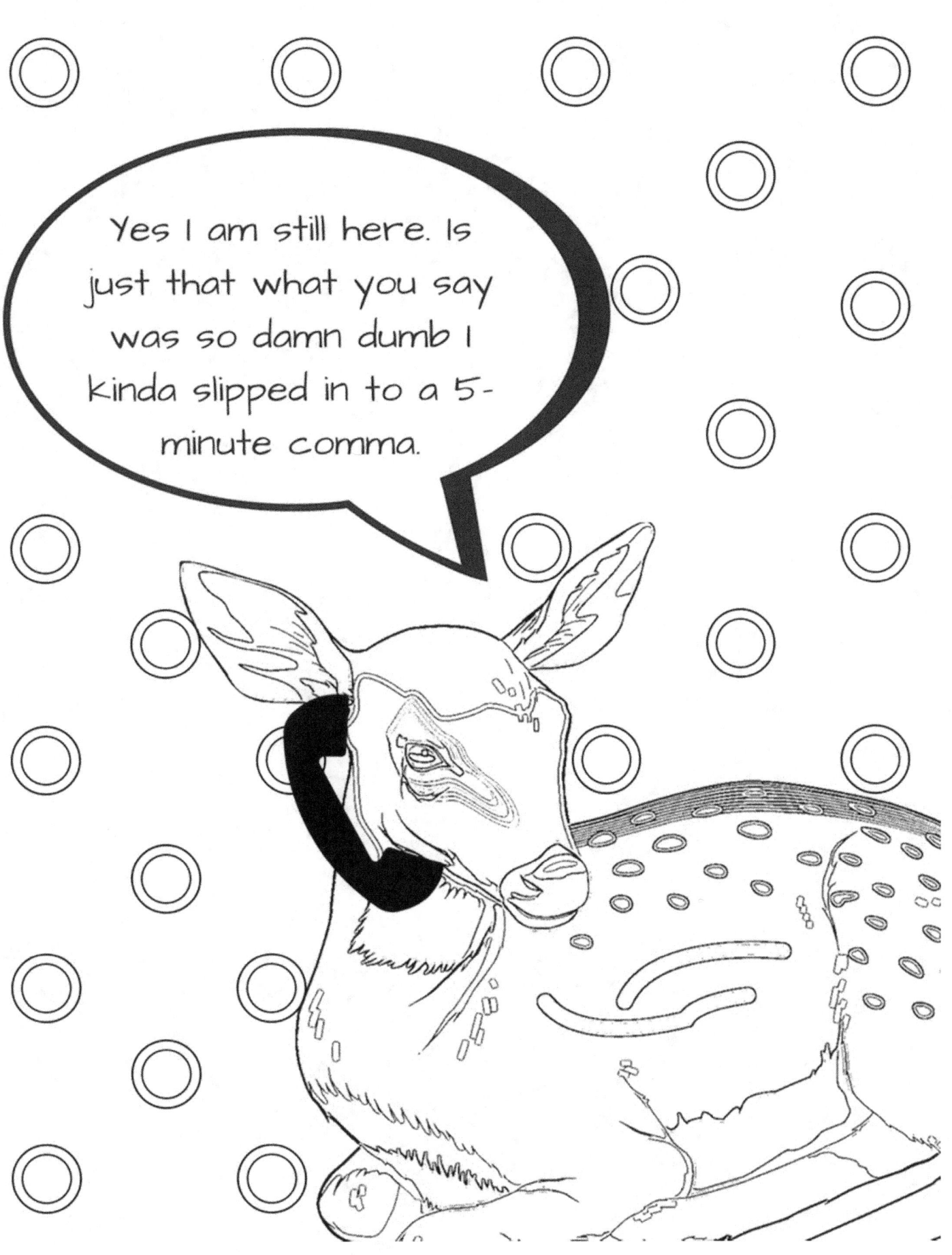

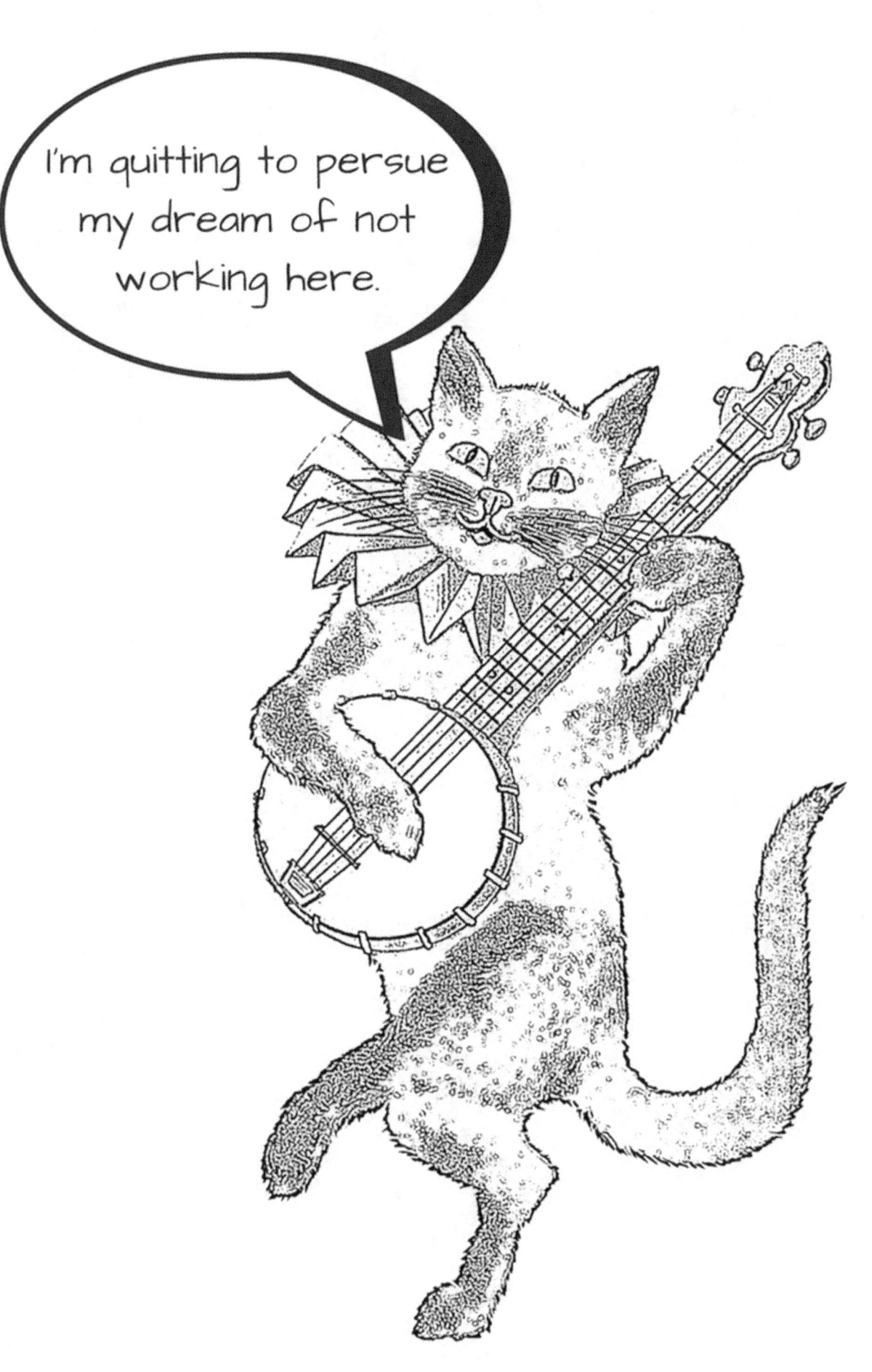

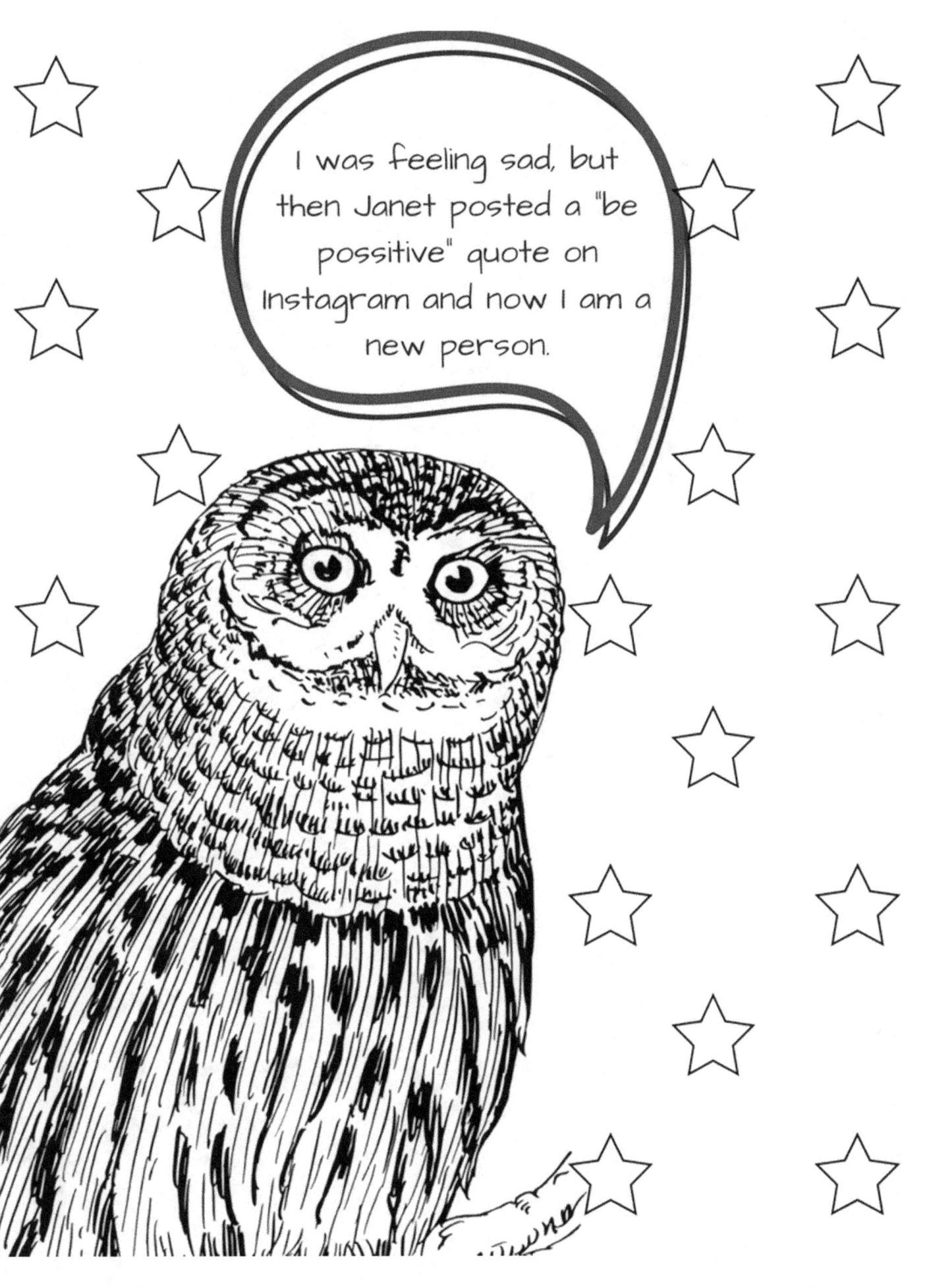

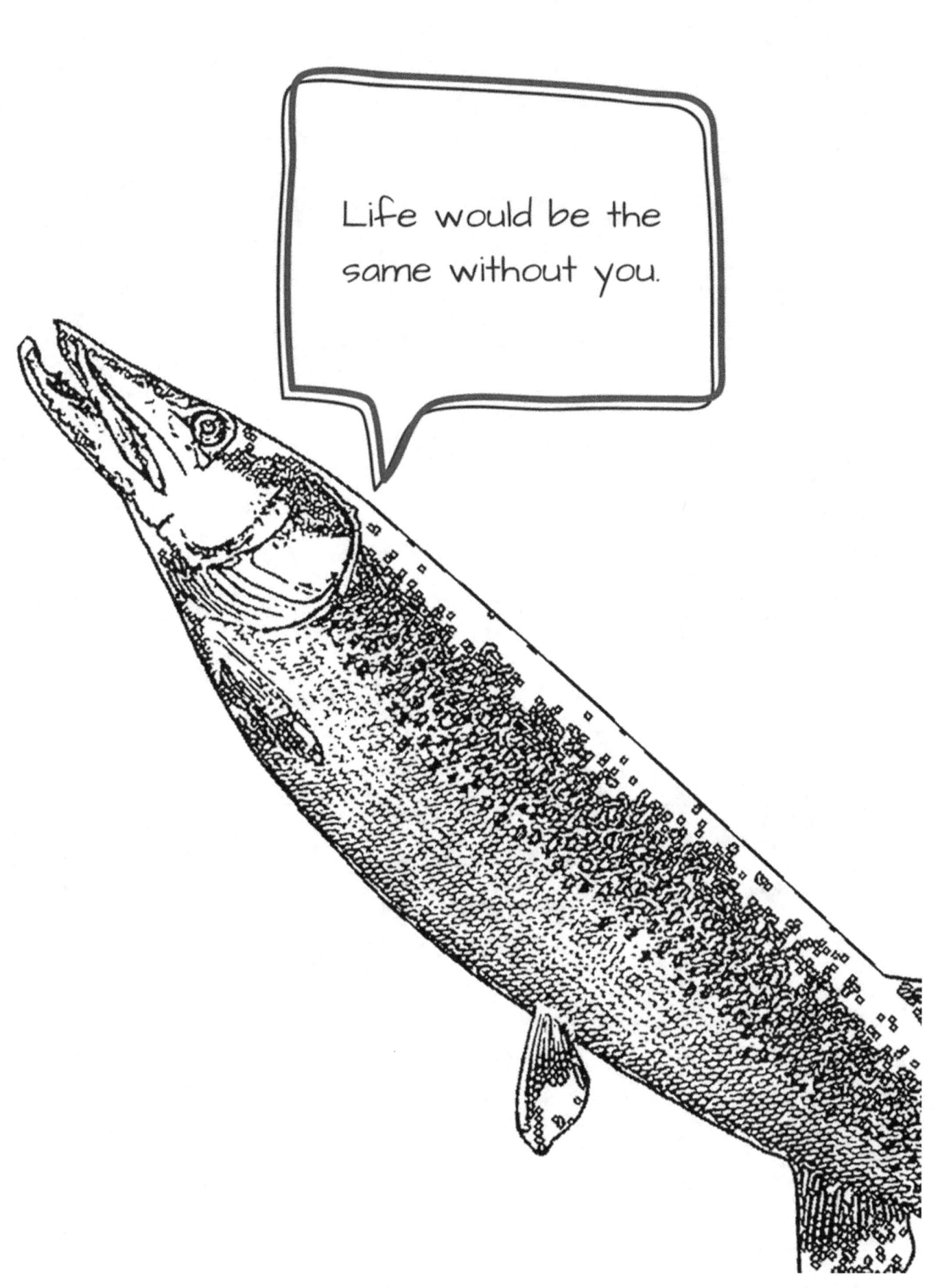

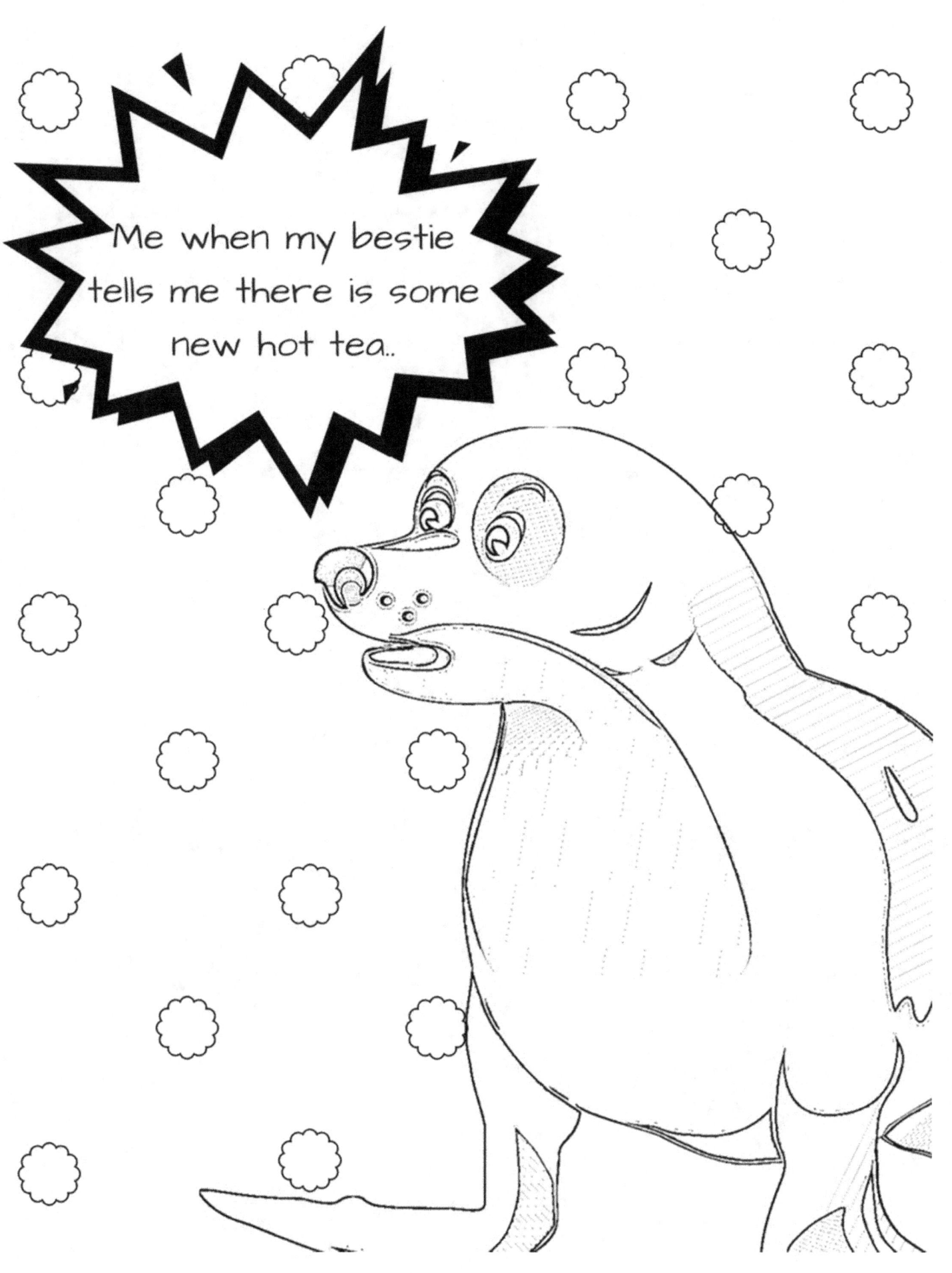

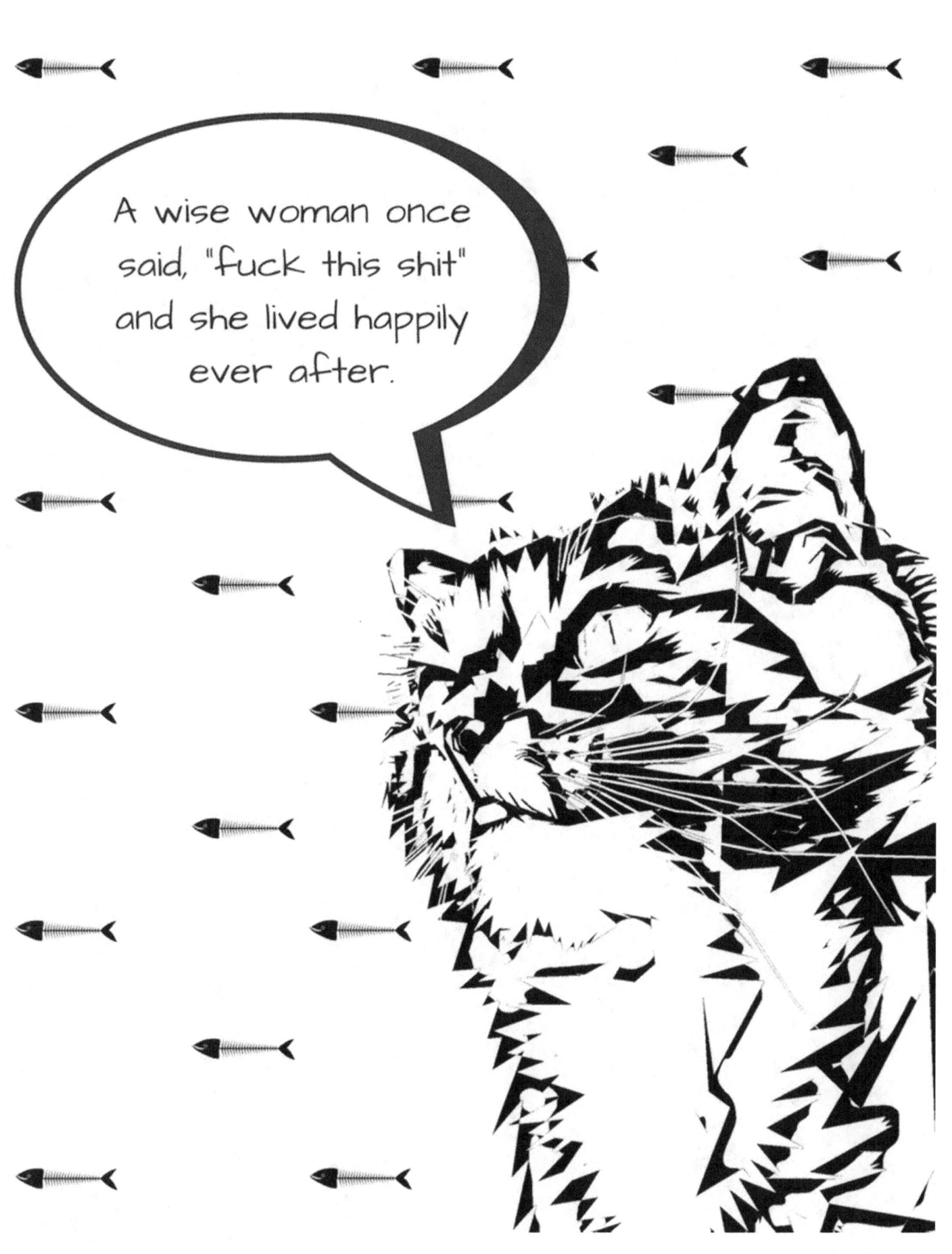

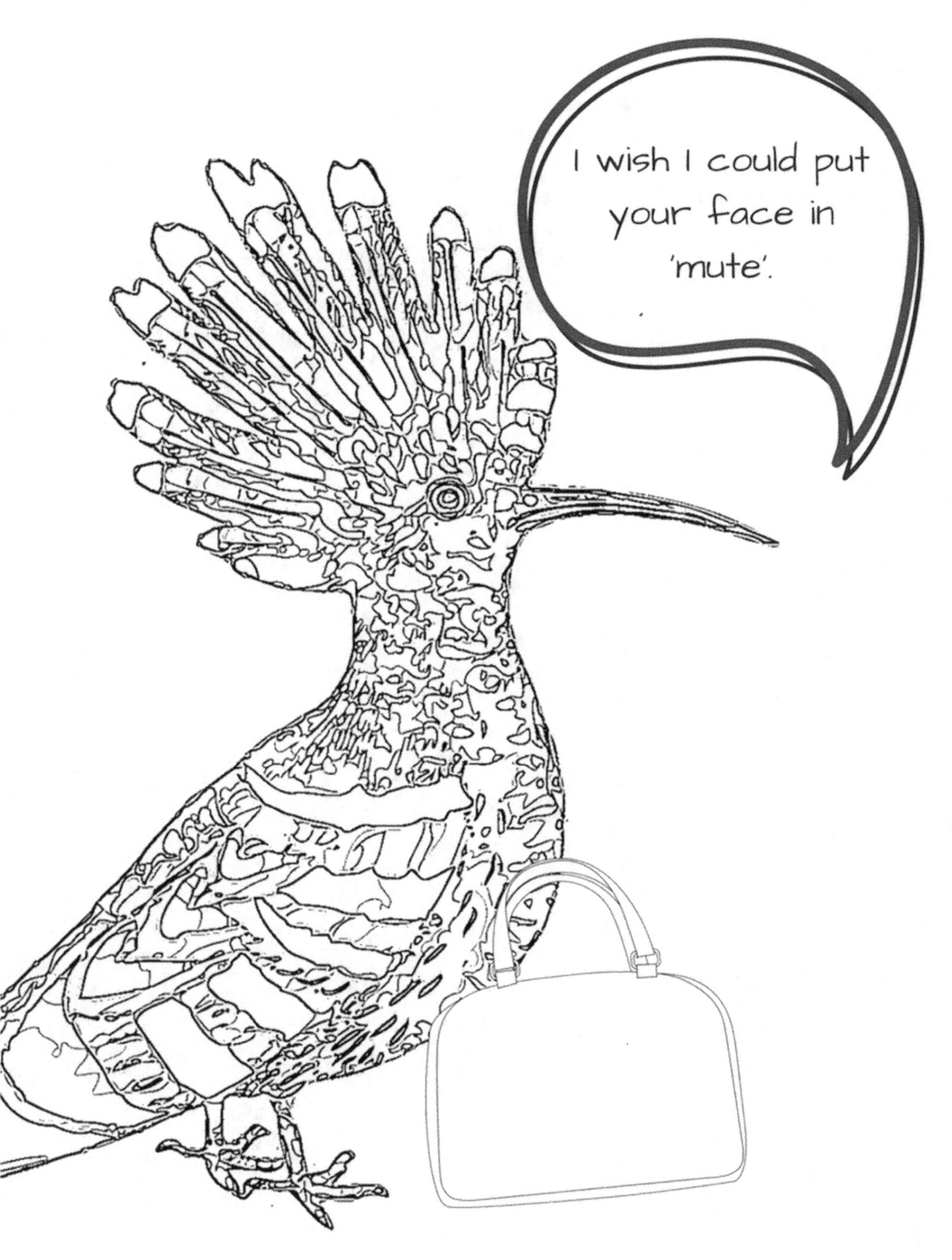

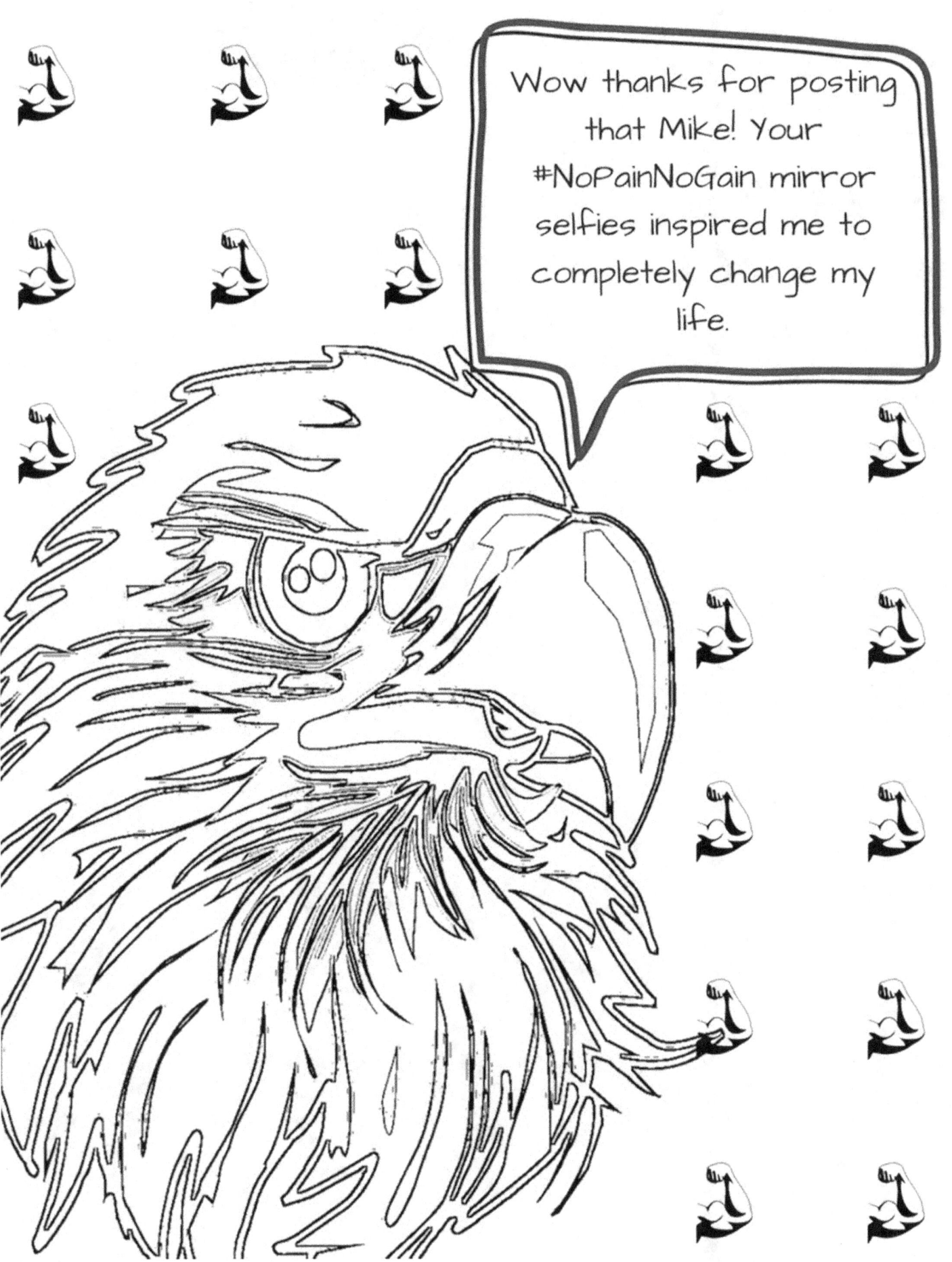

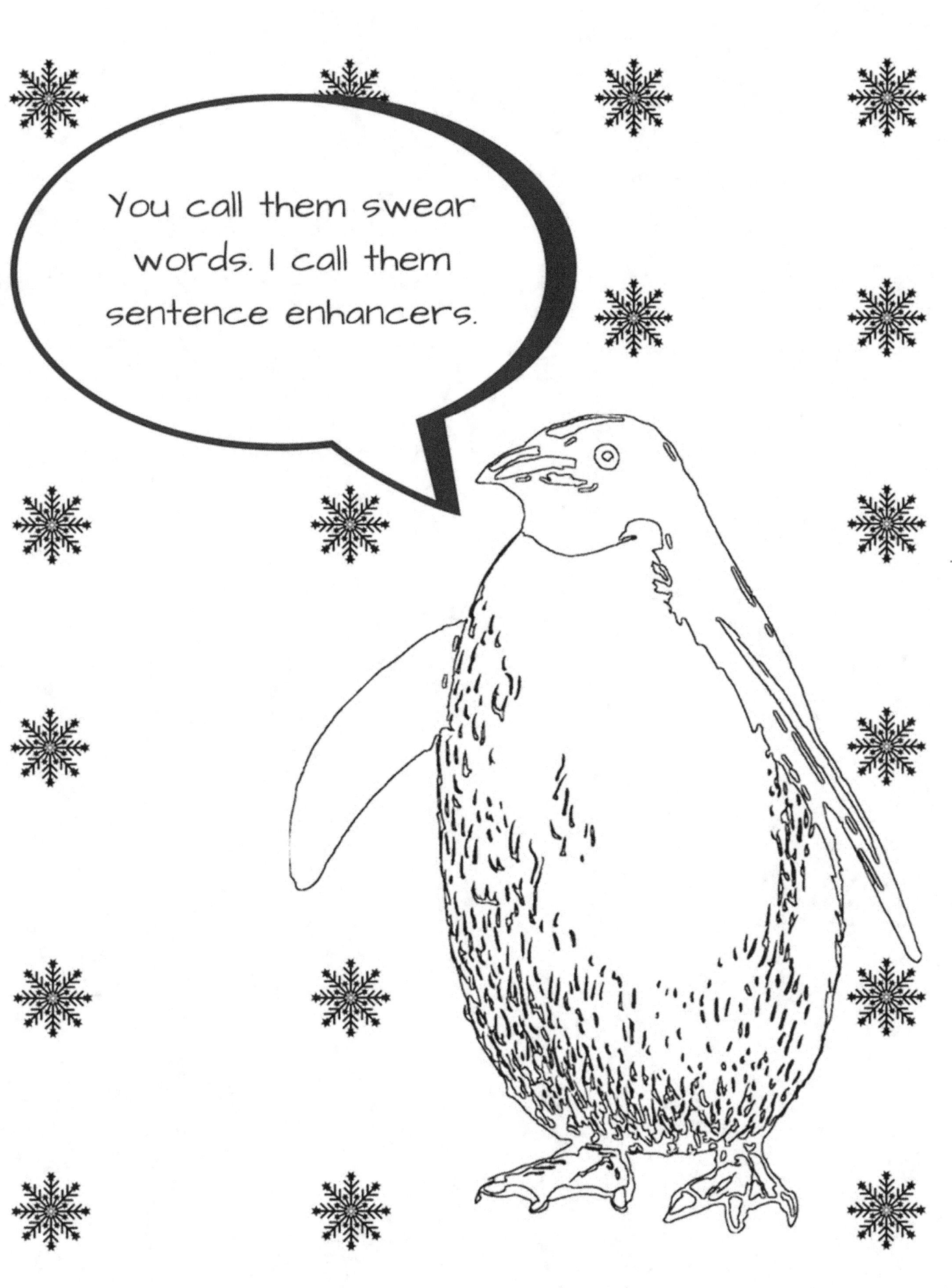

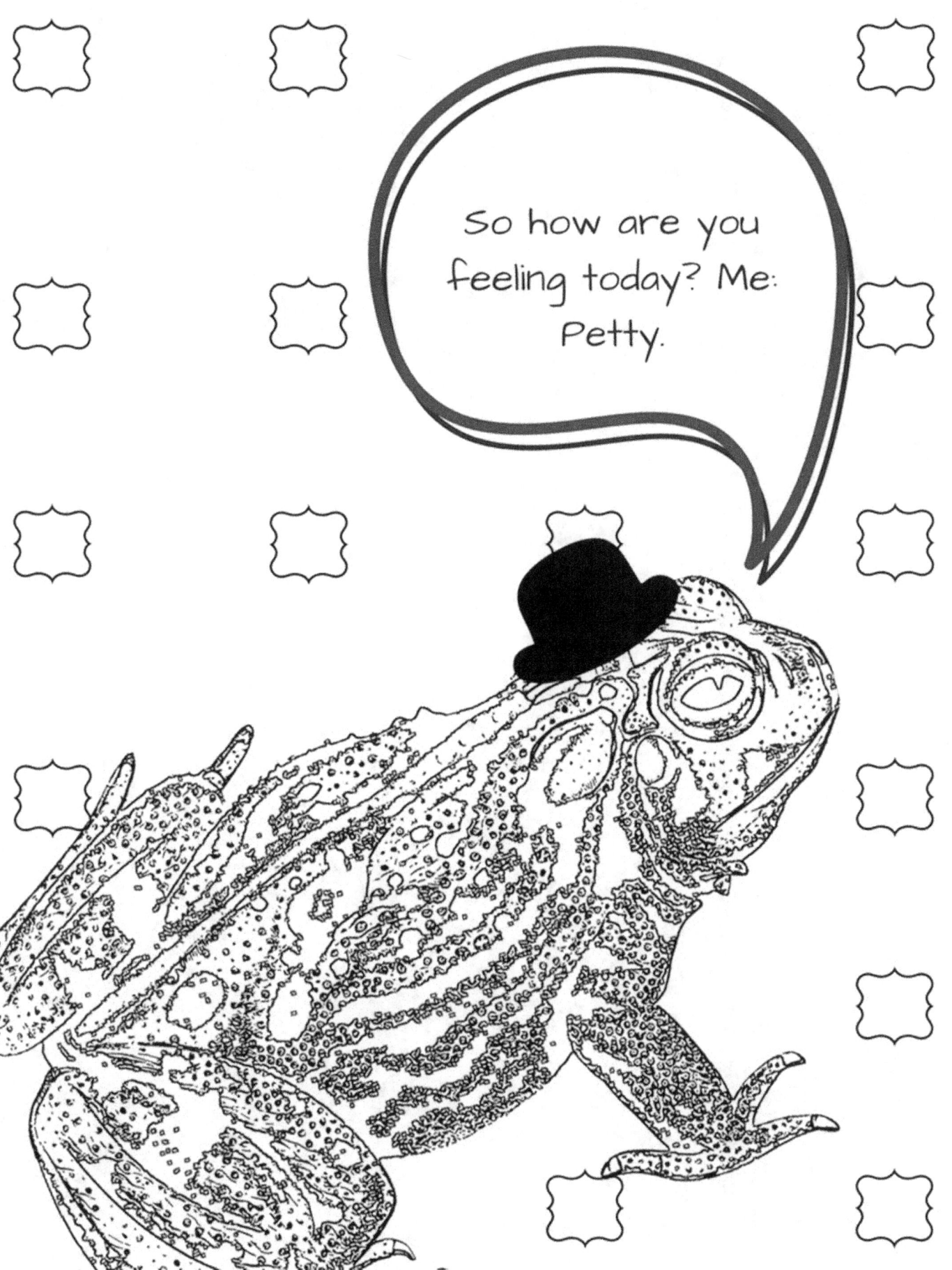

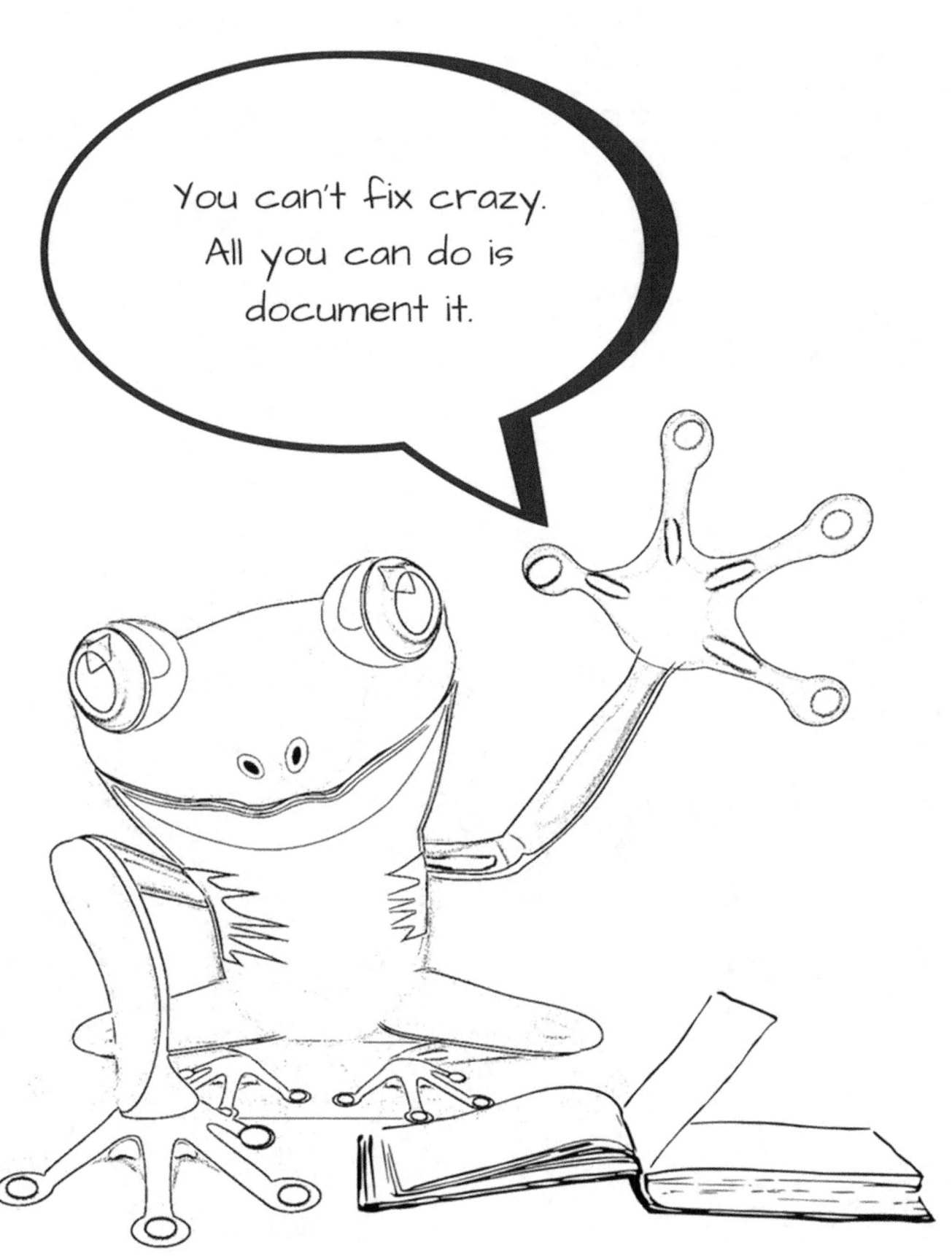

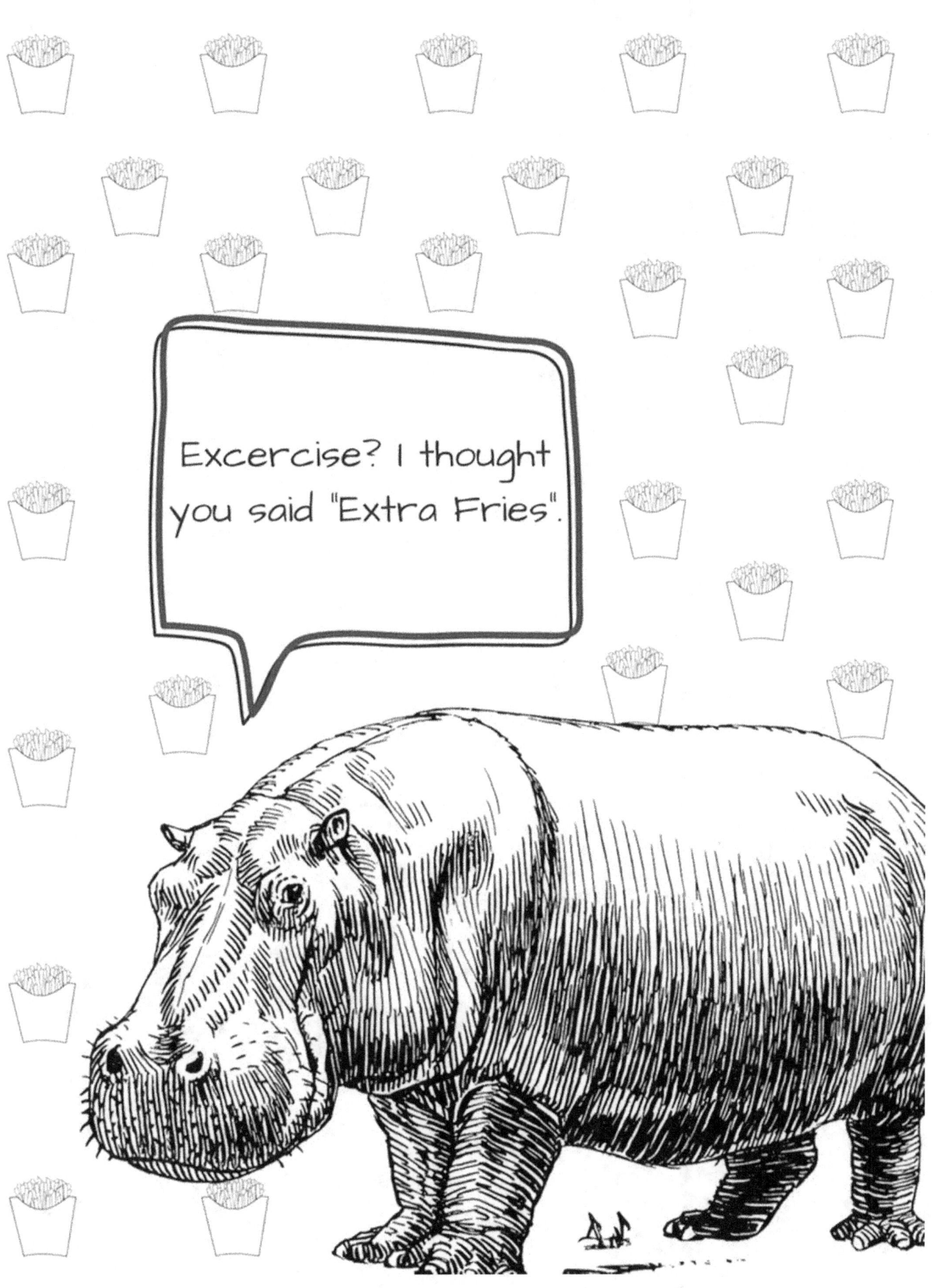

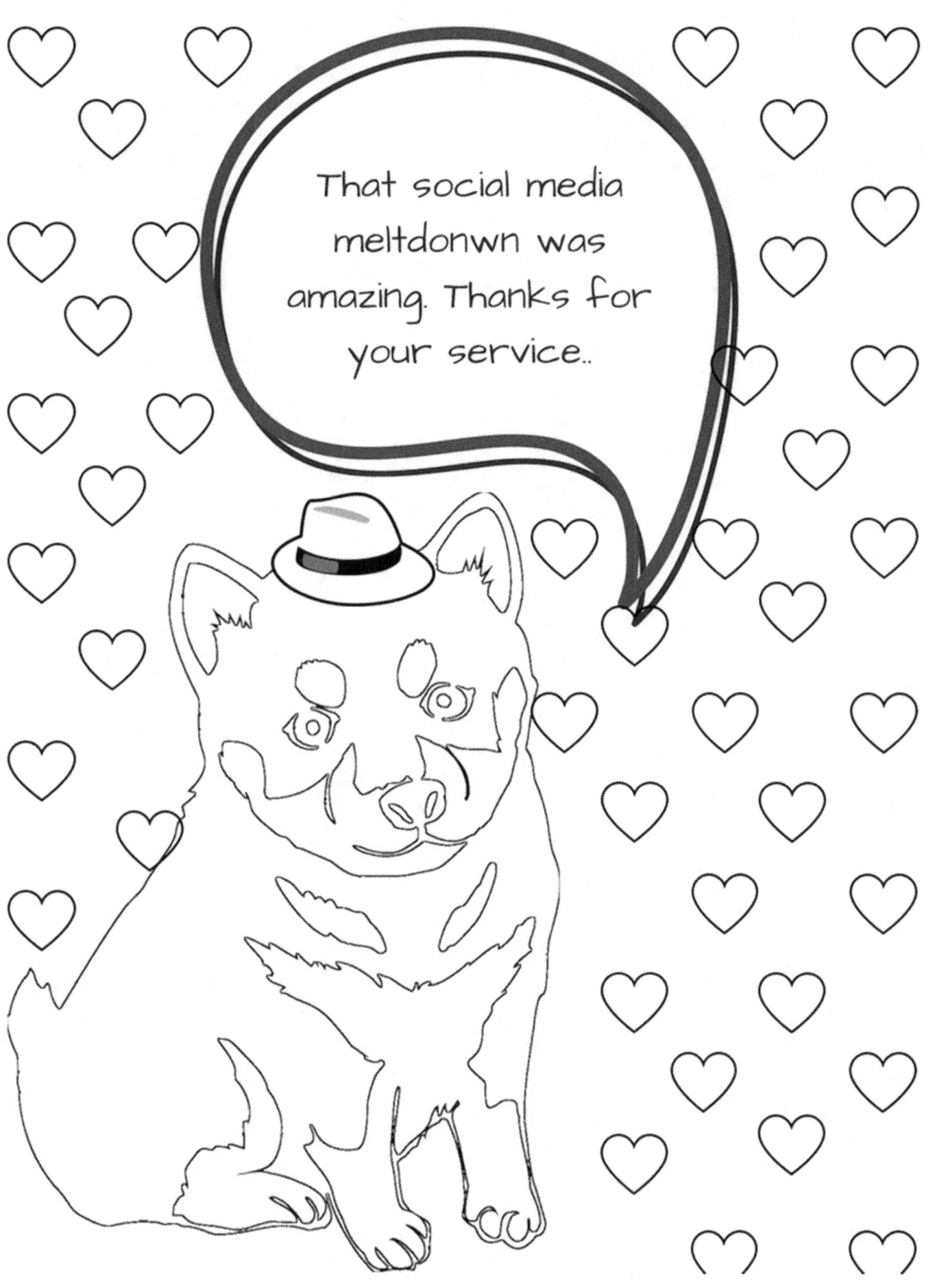

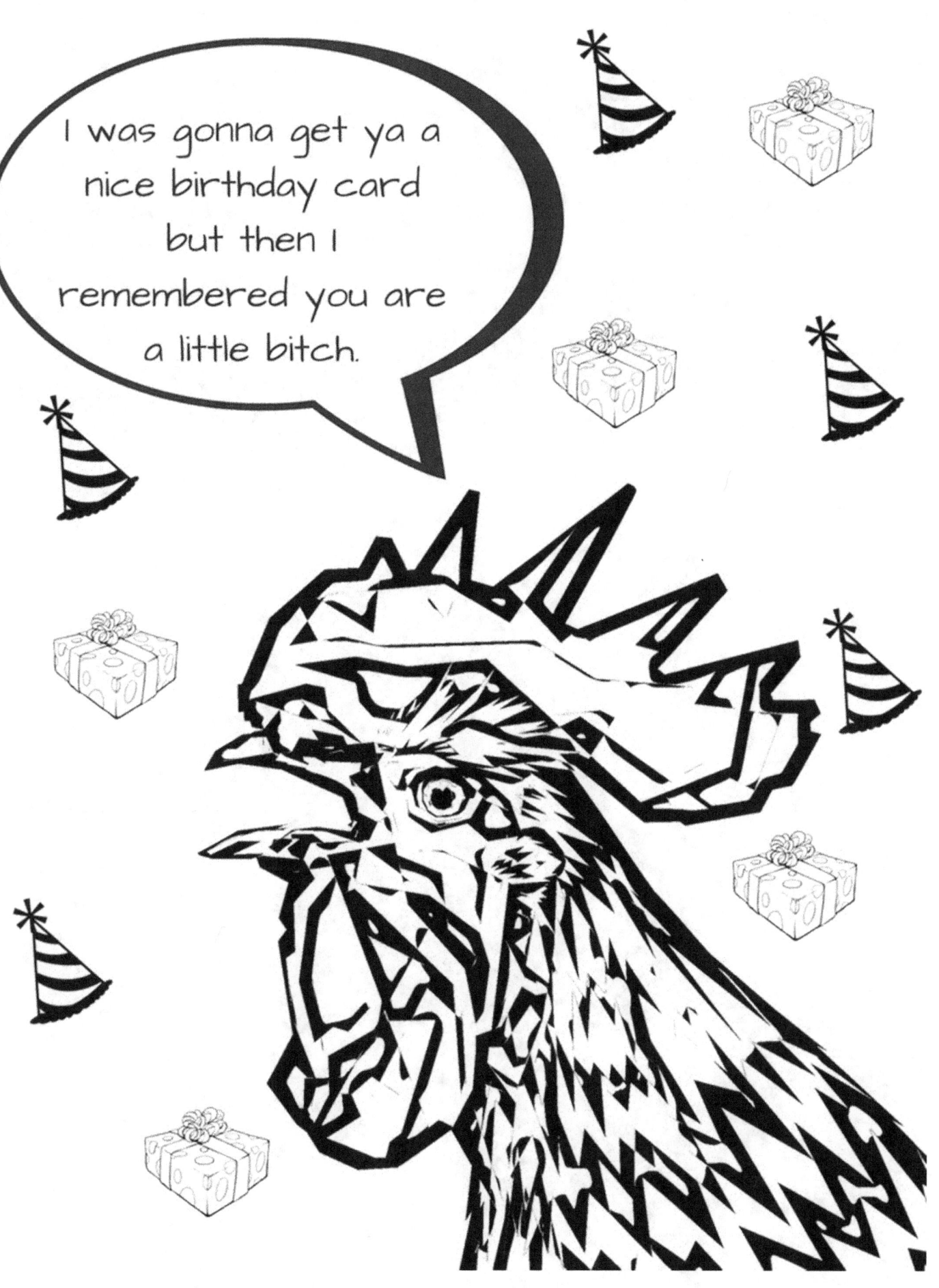

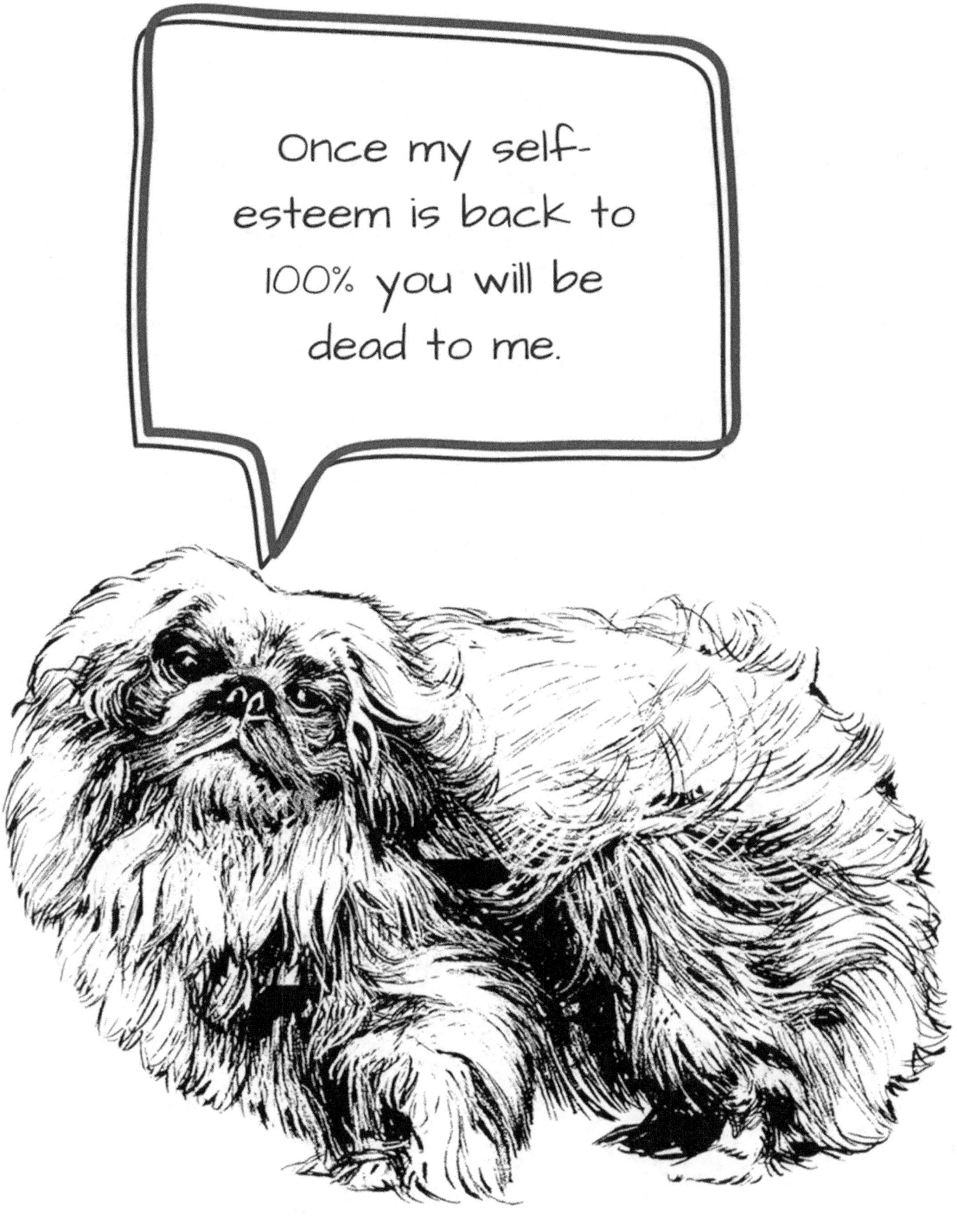

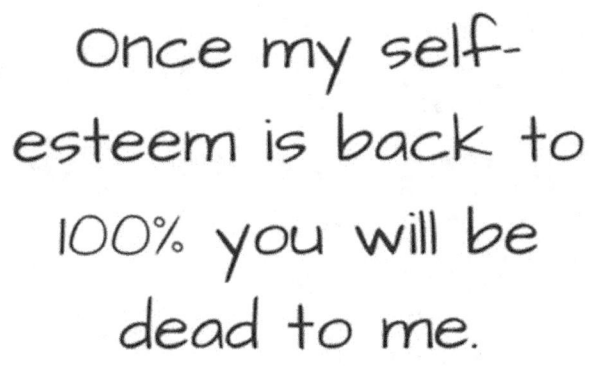

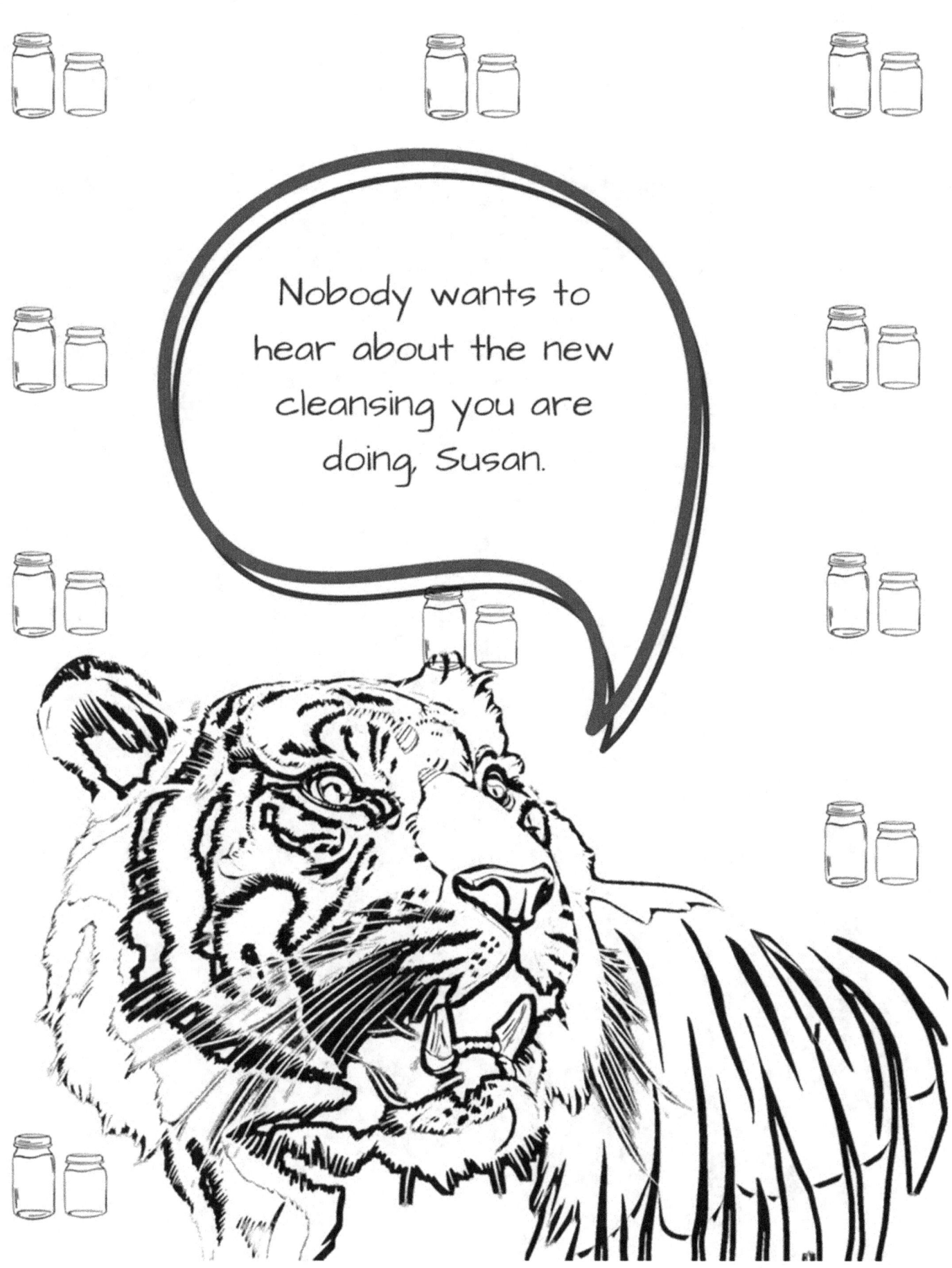

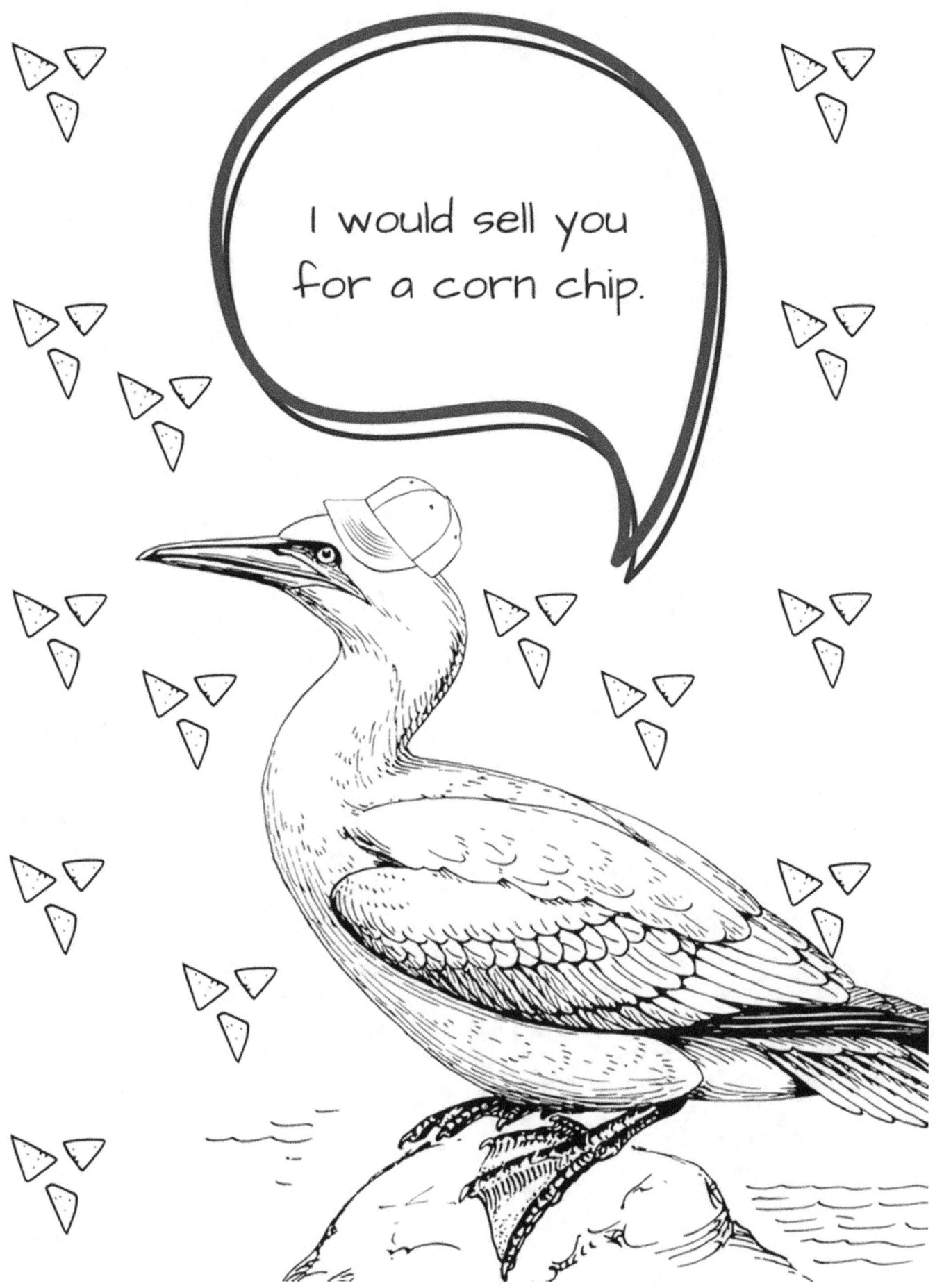

I wish you were
a piñata.

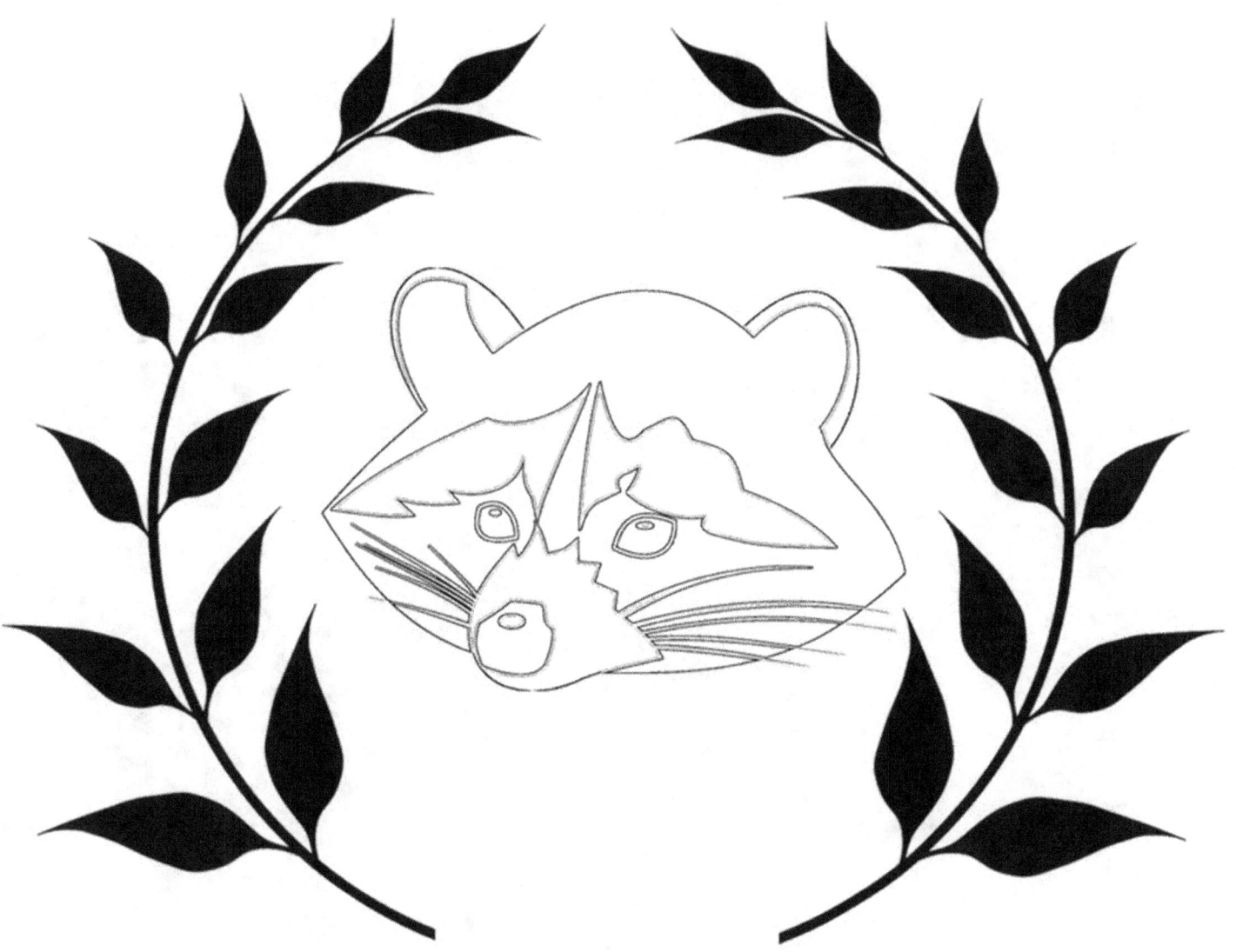

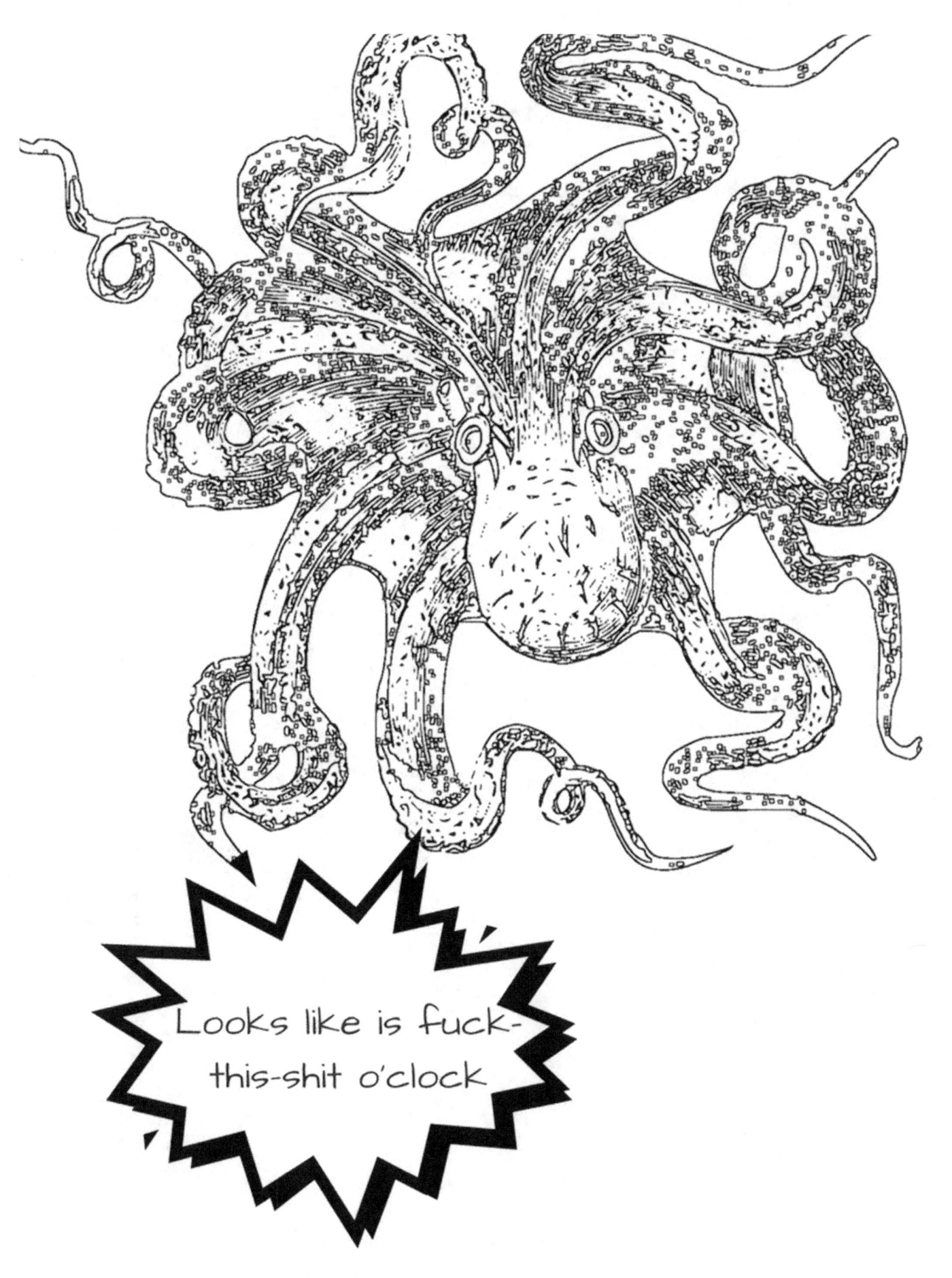

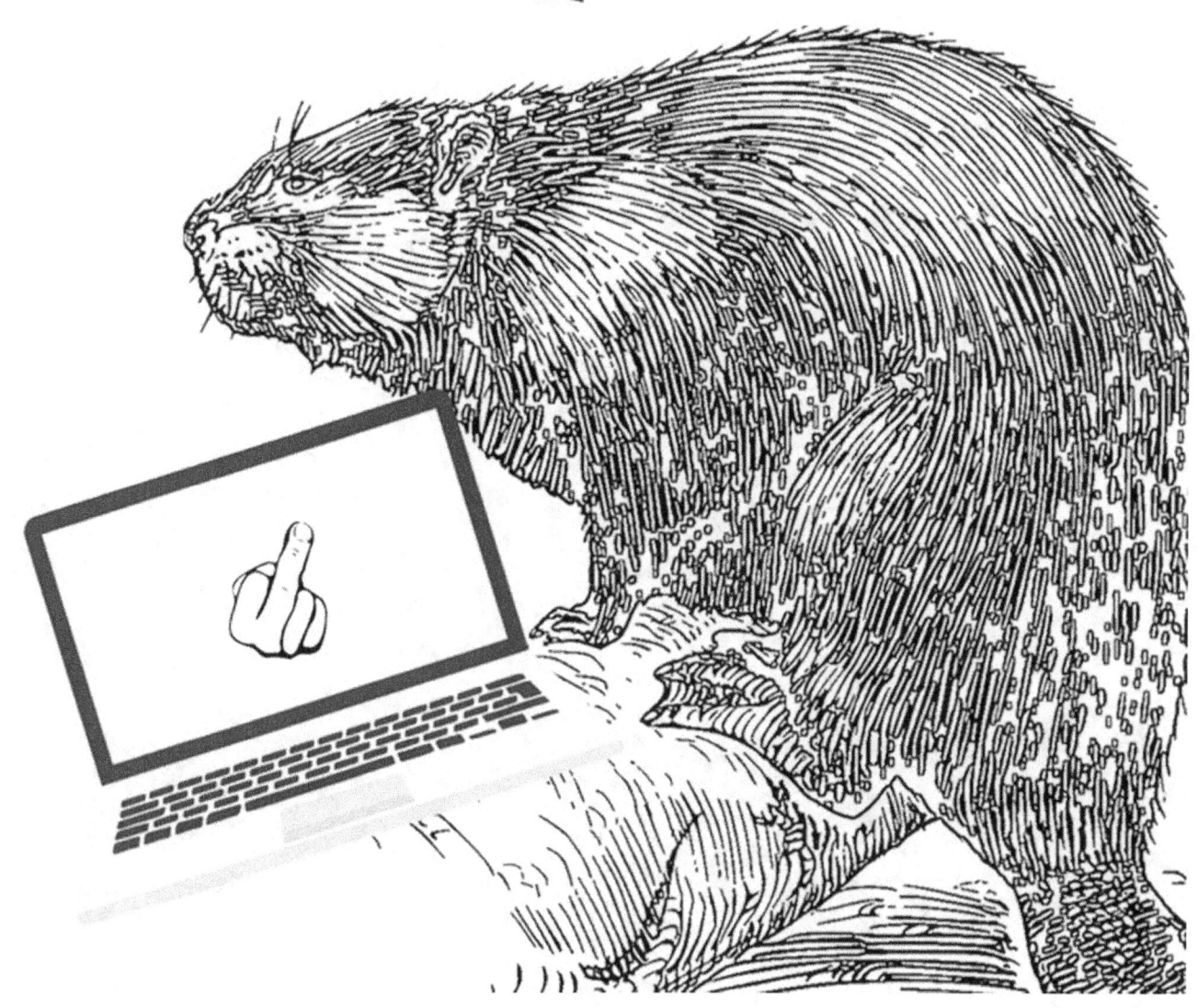

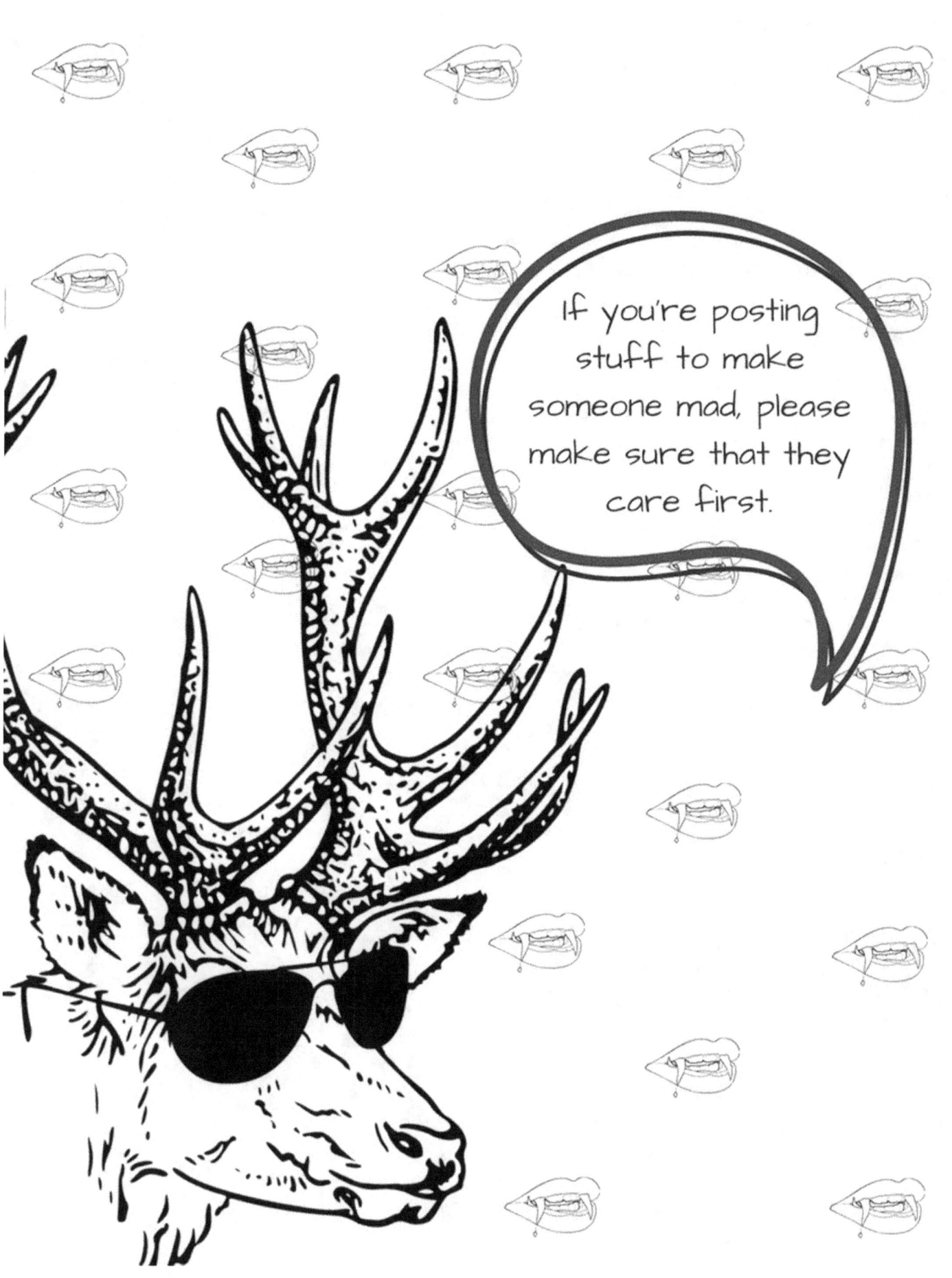

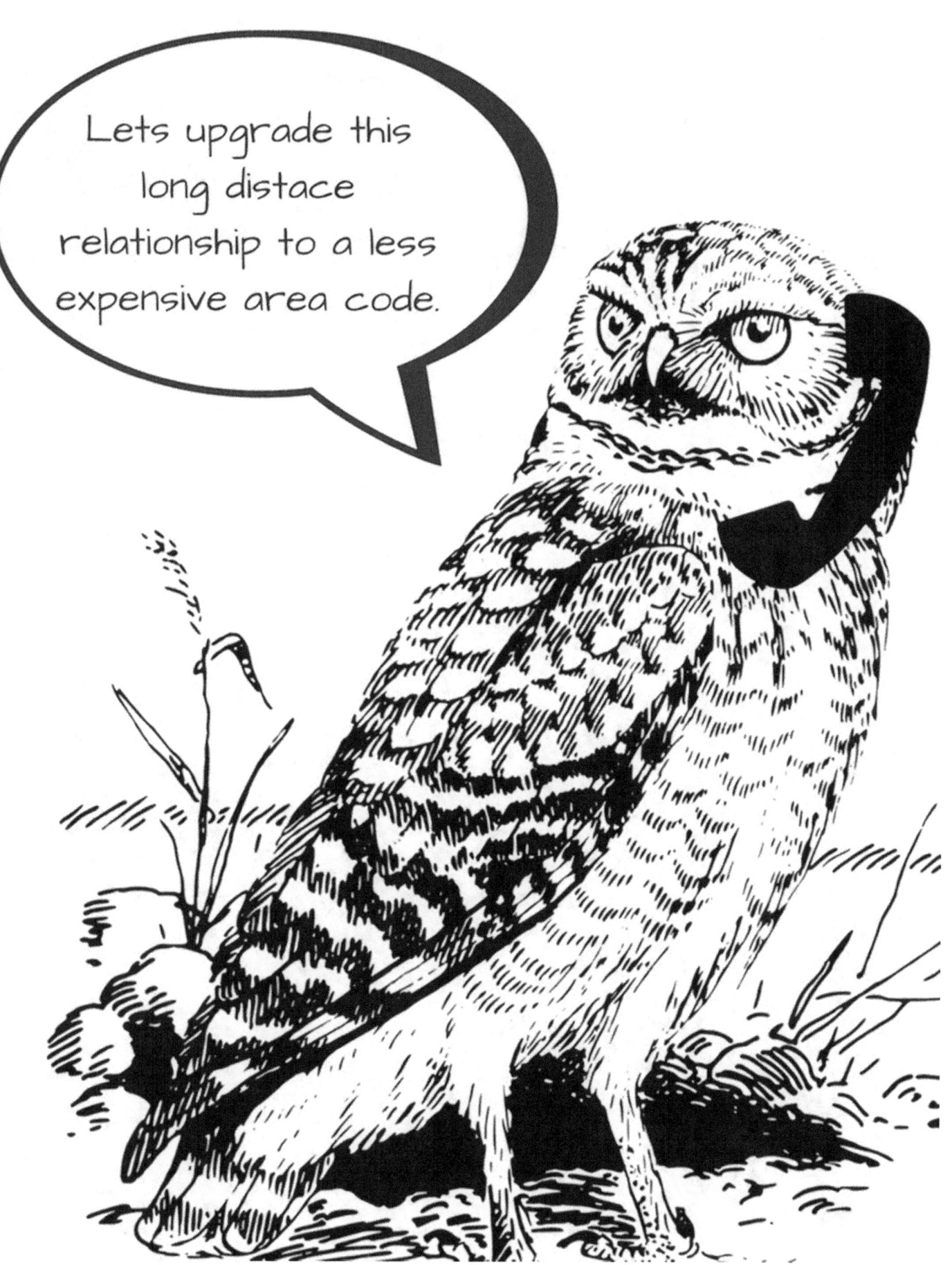

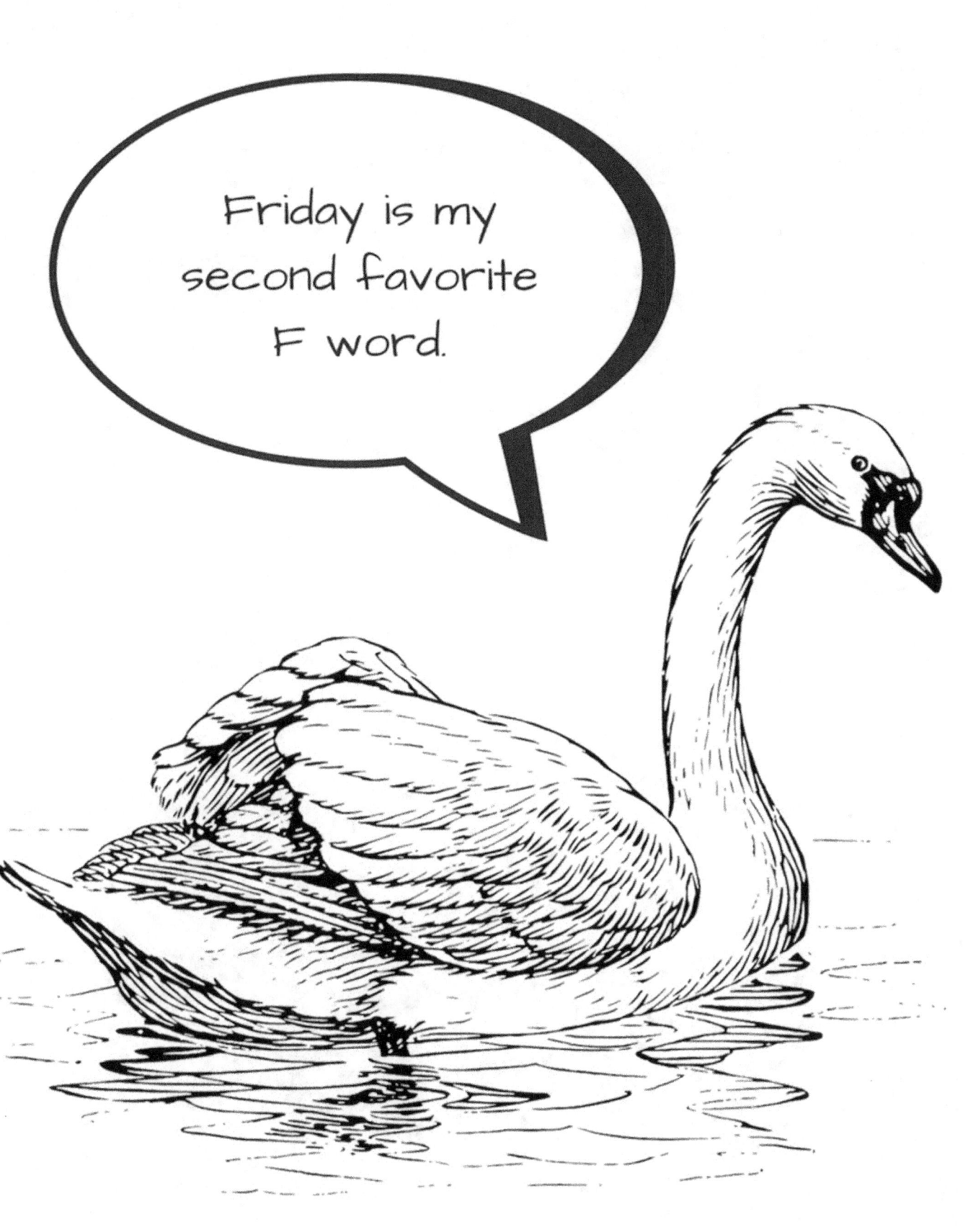

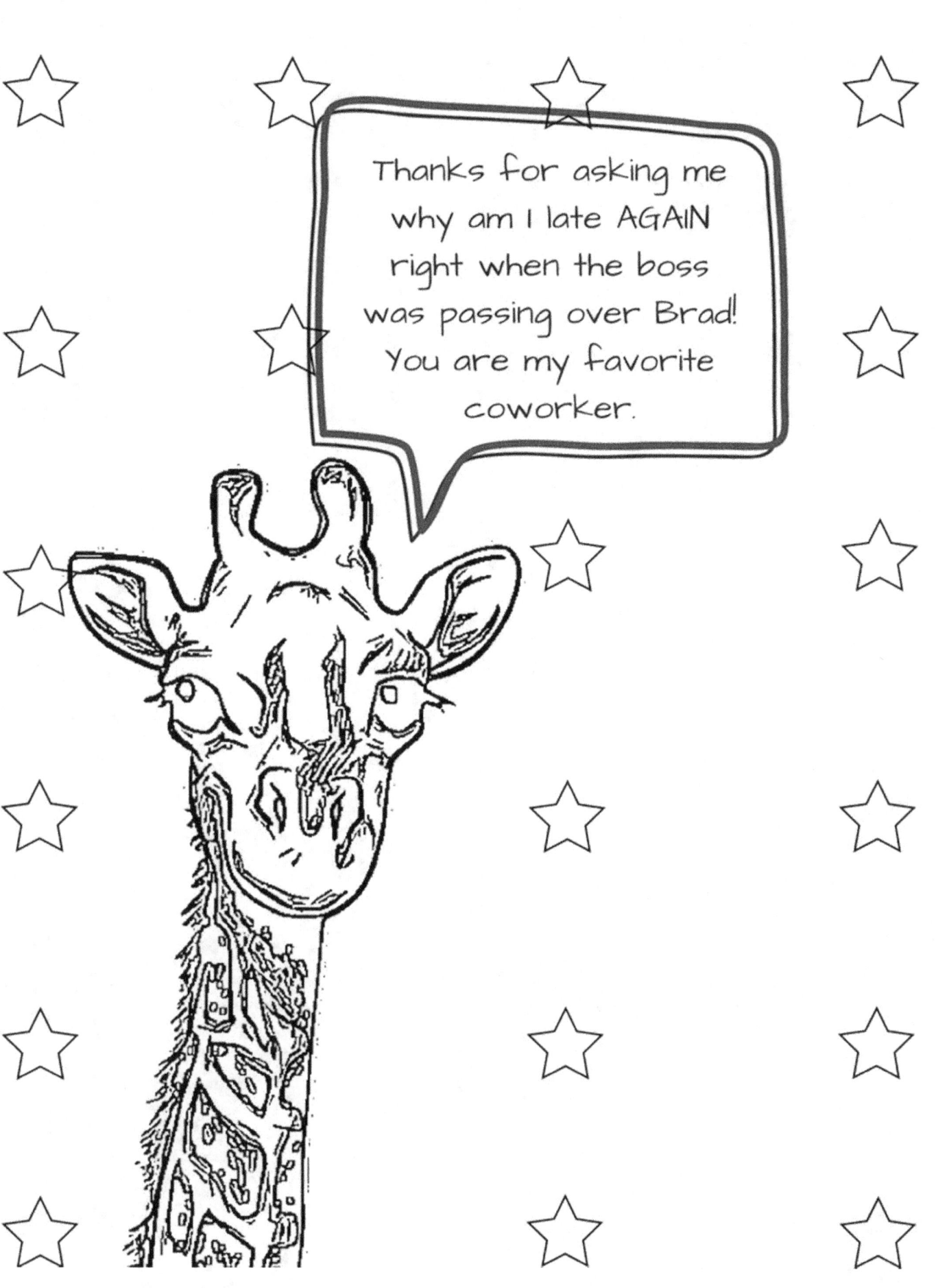

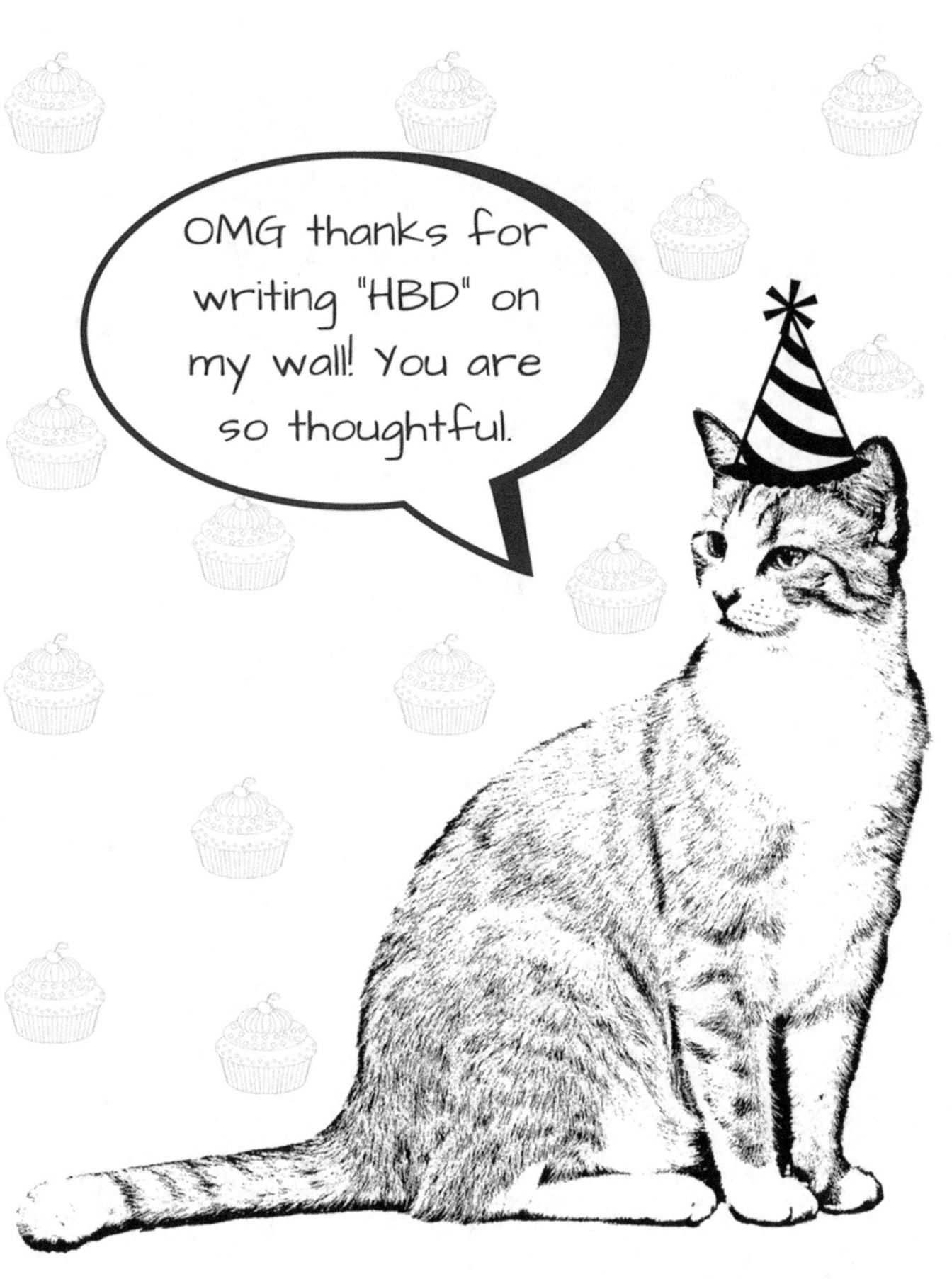

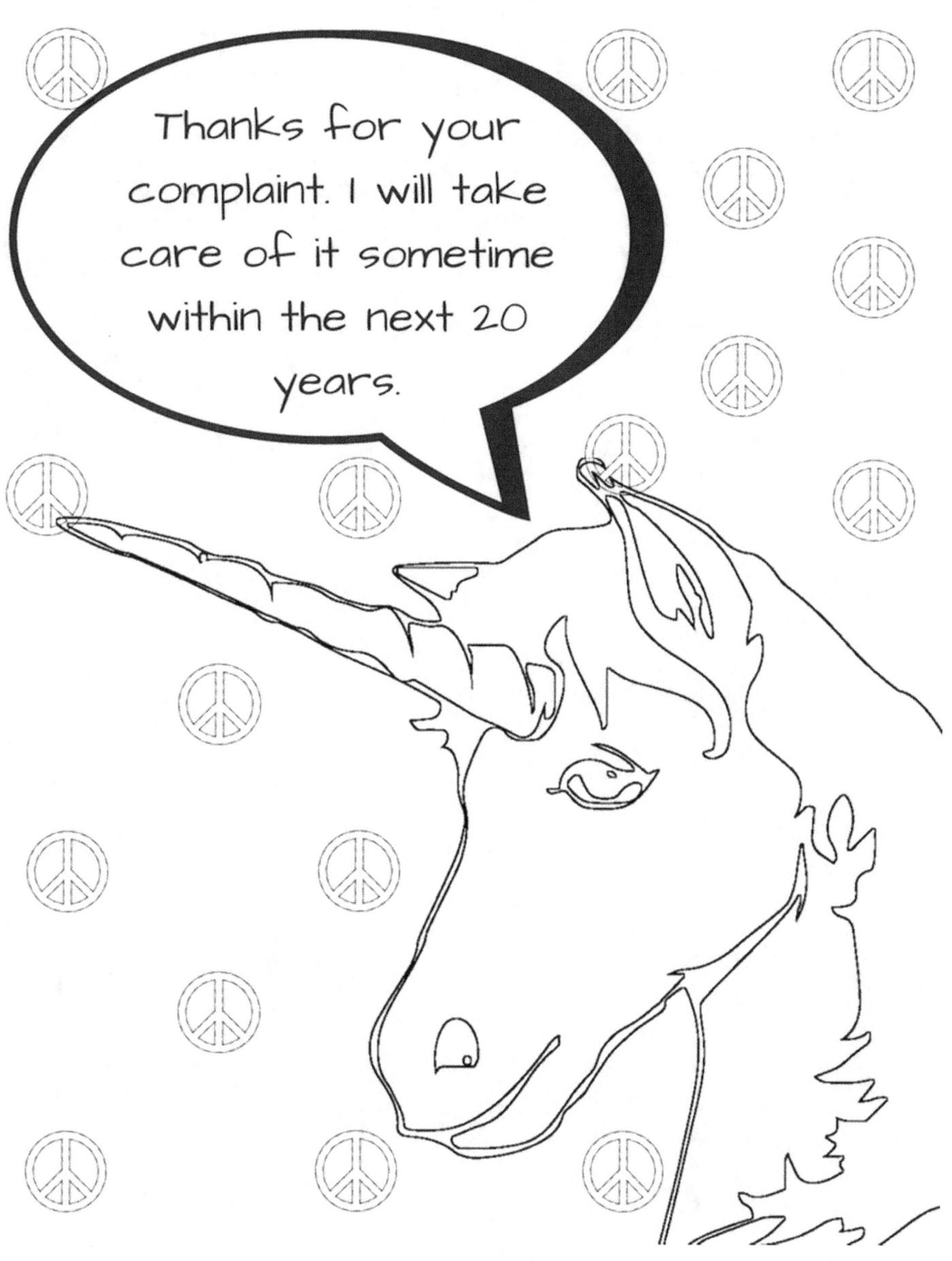

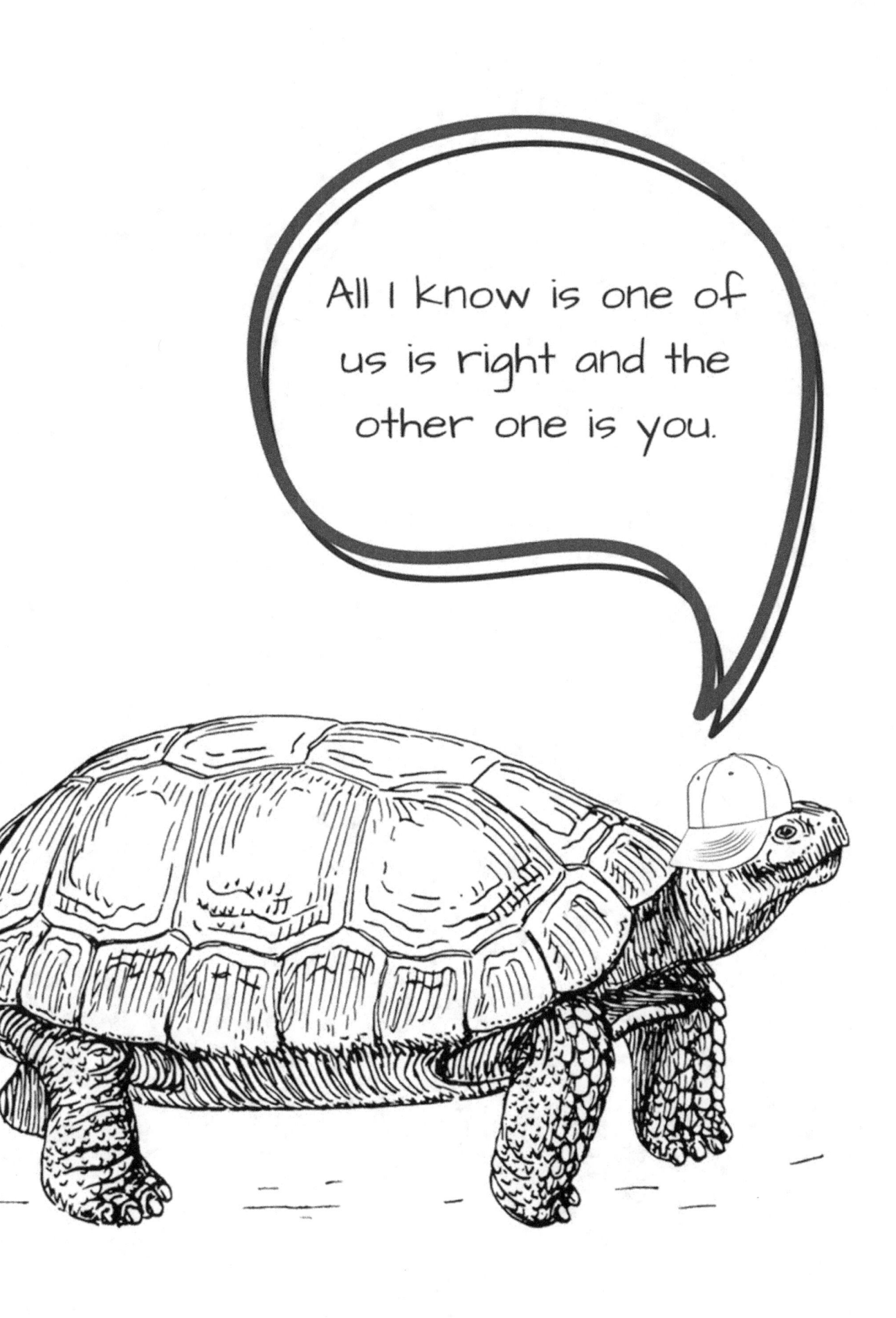

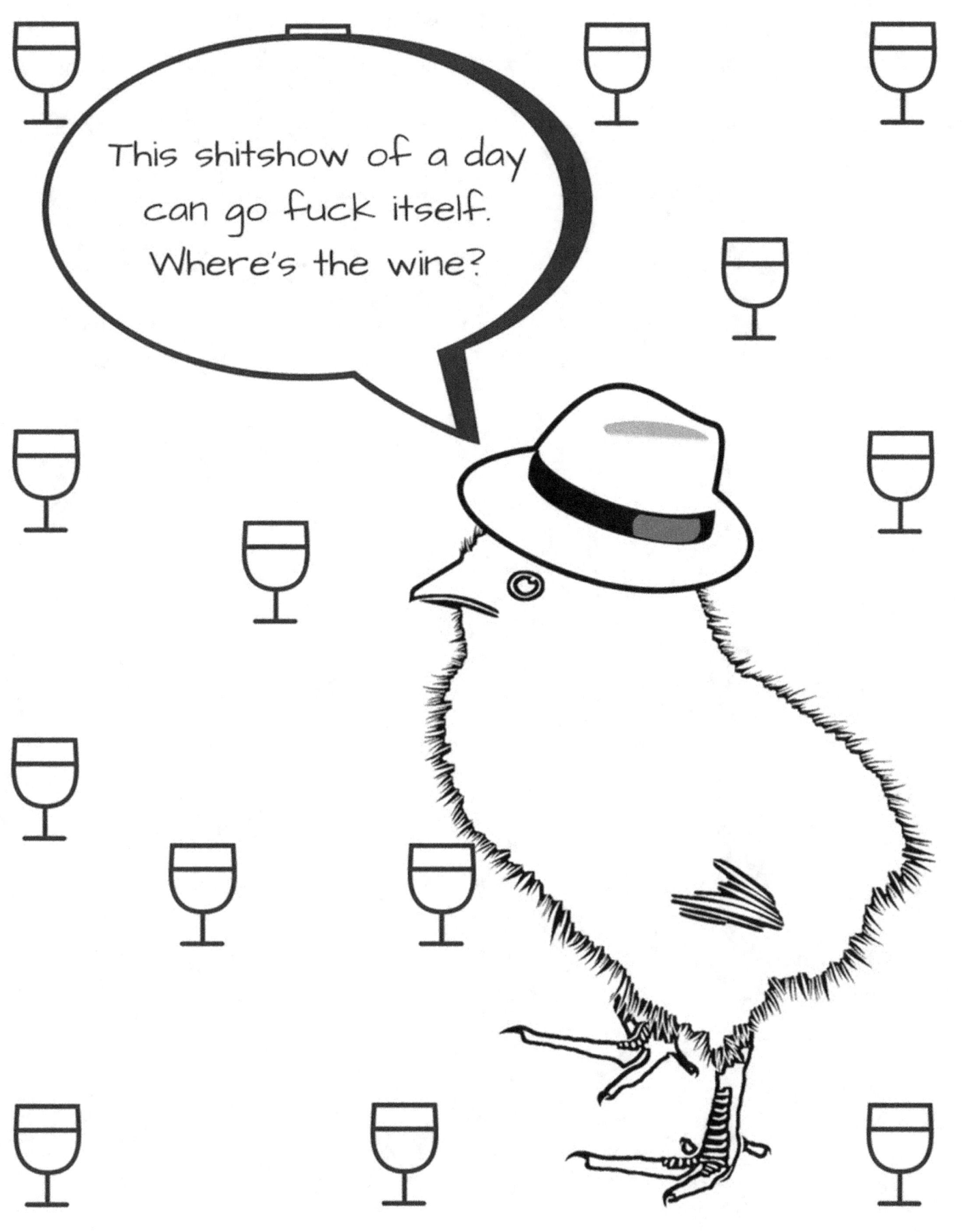

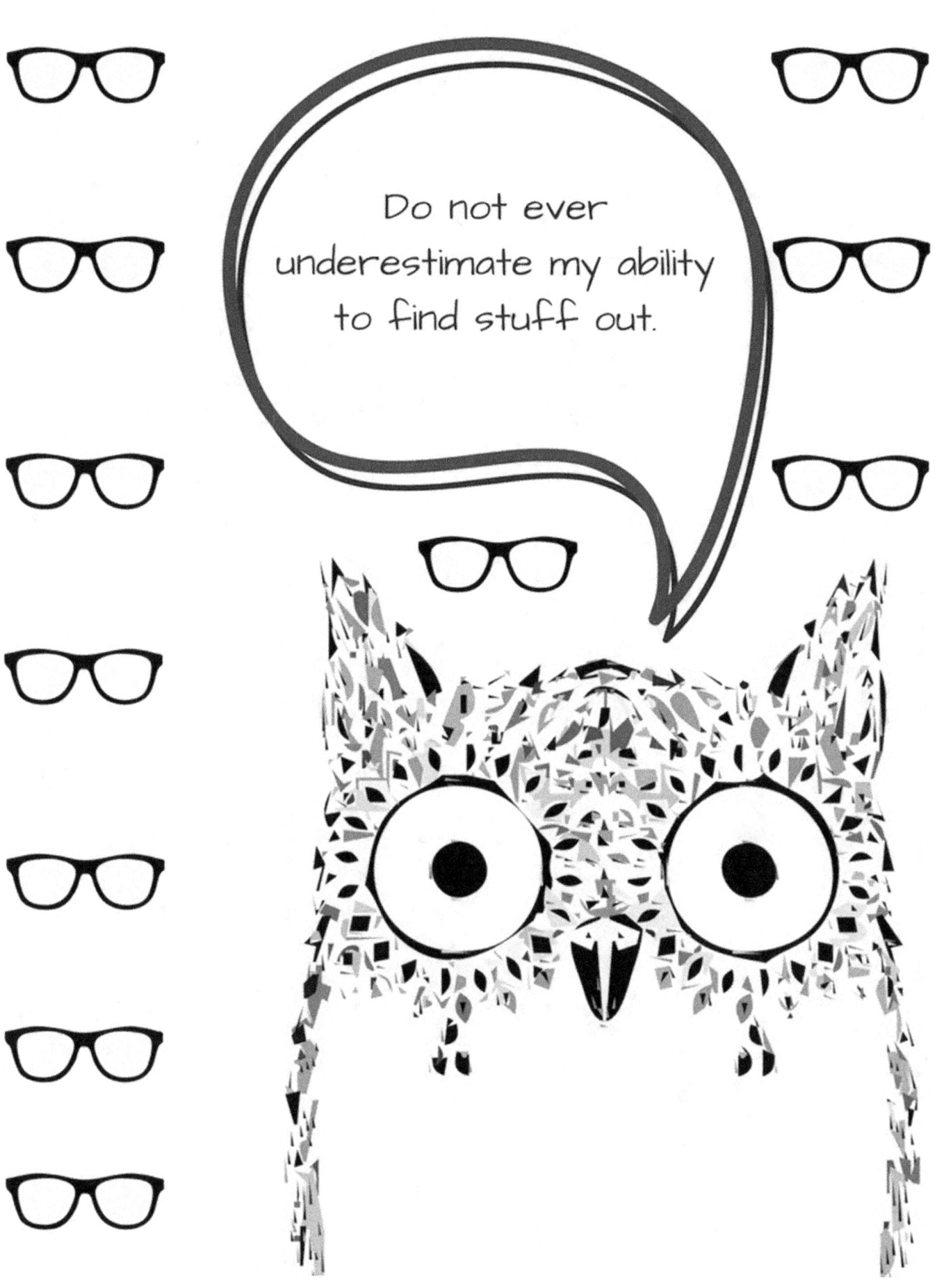

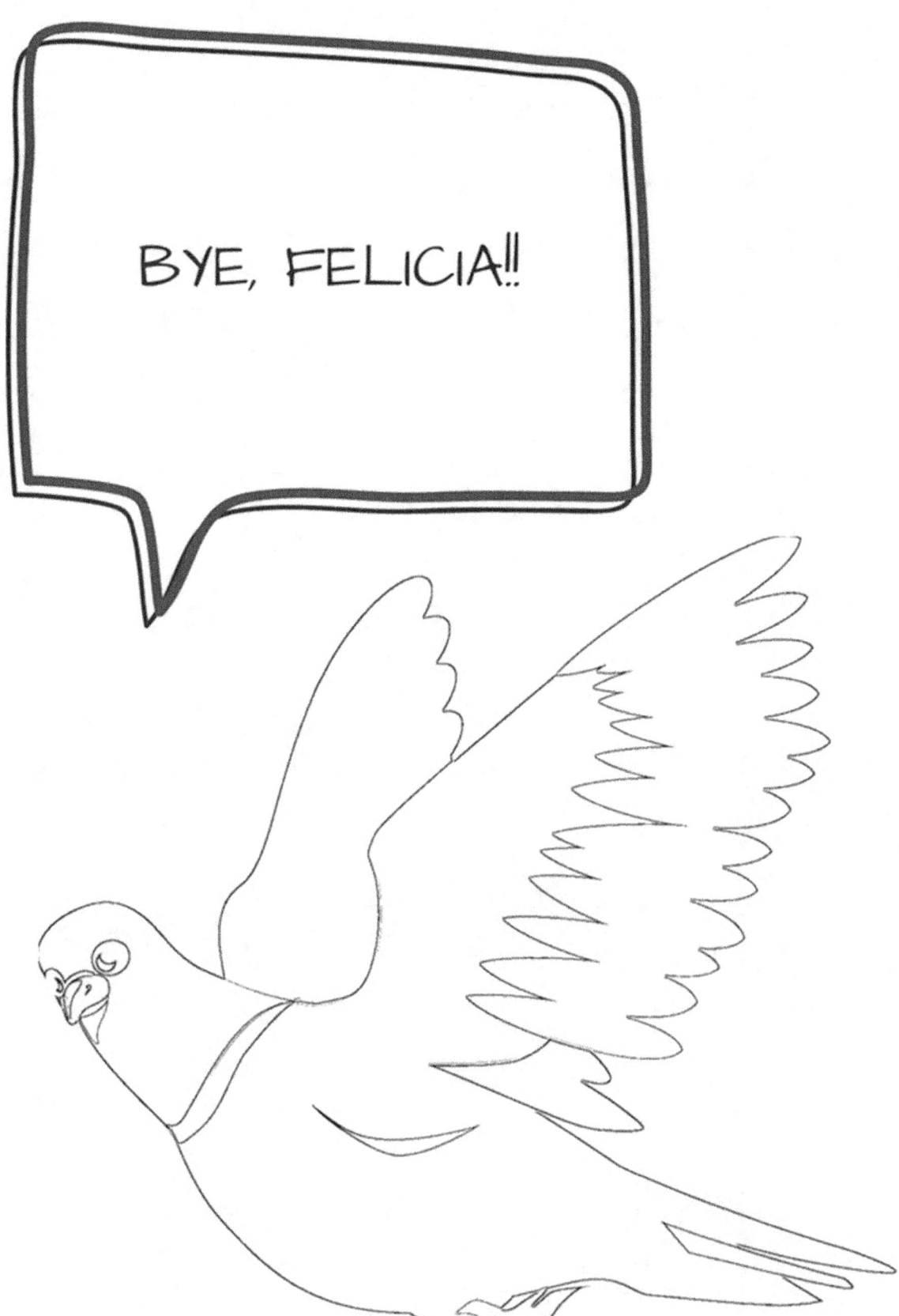

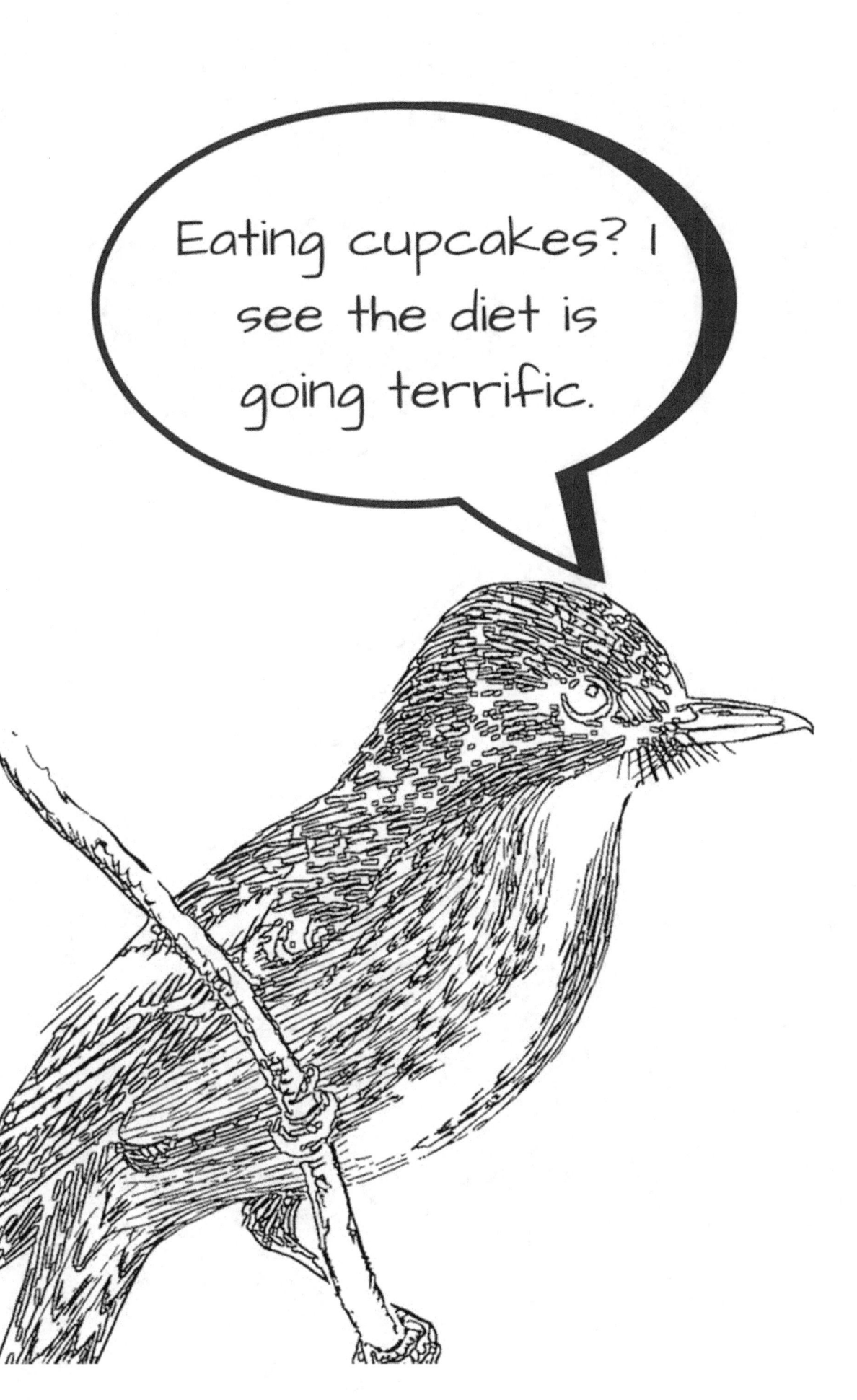

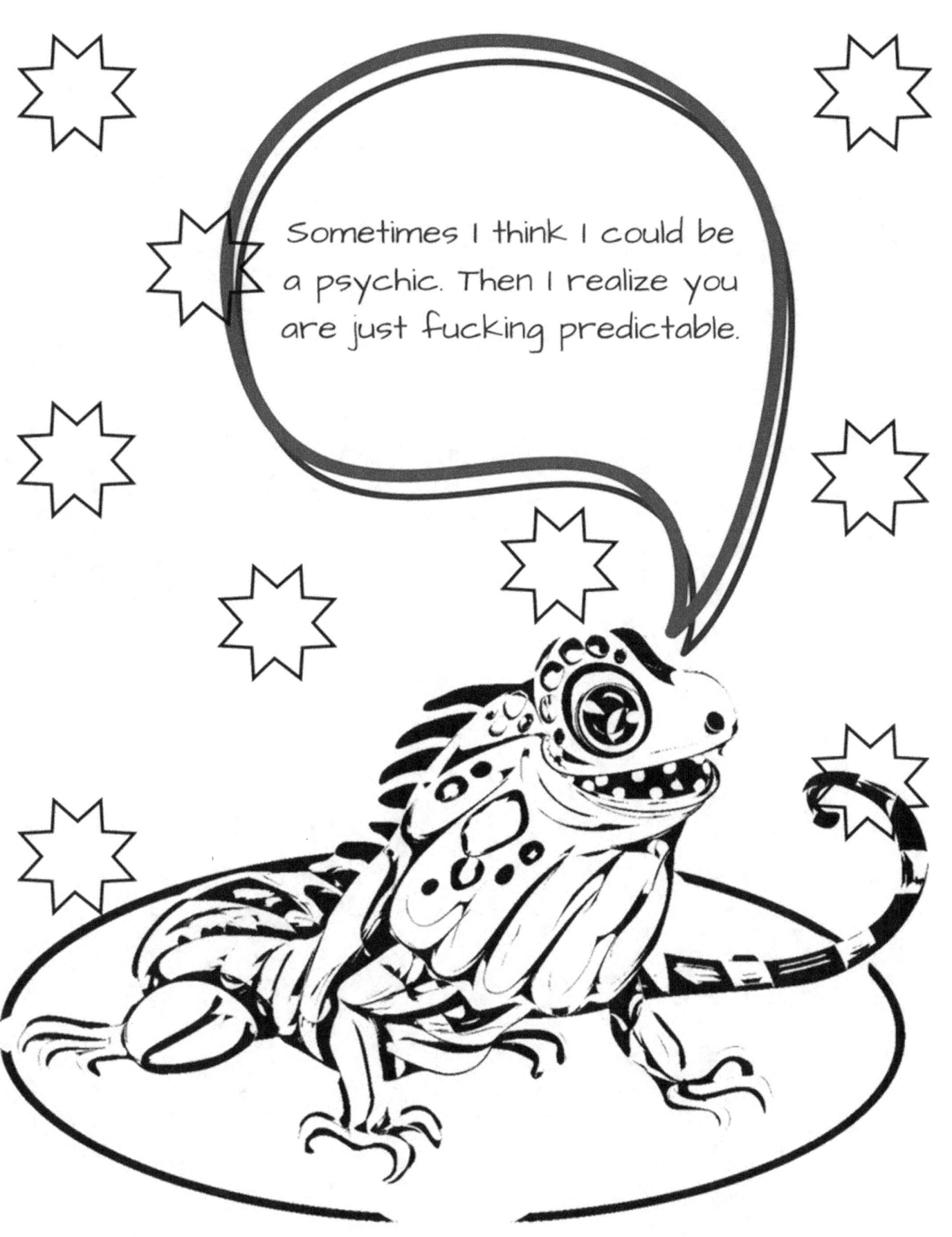

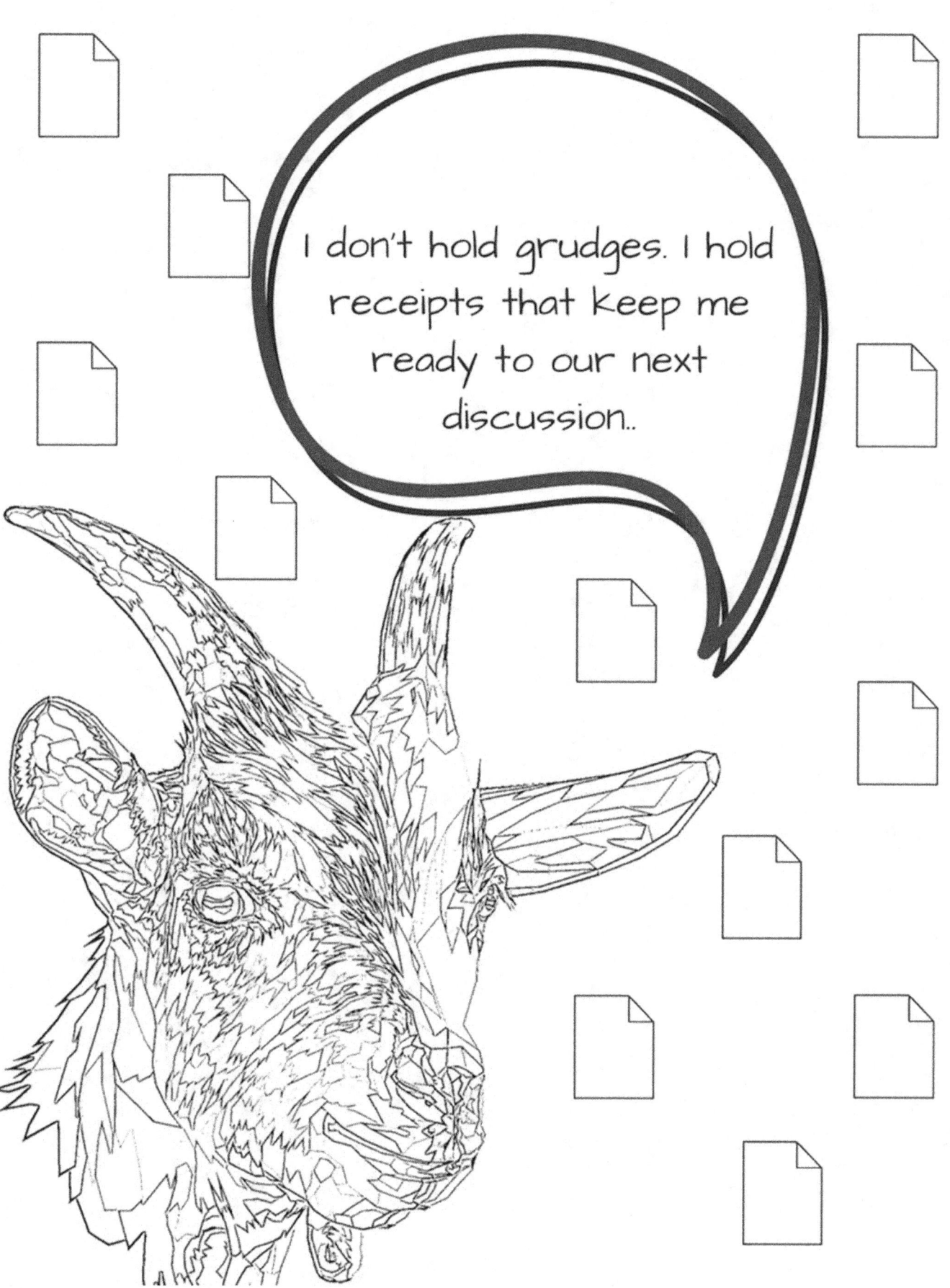

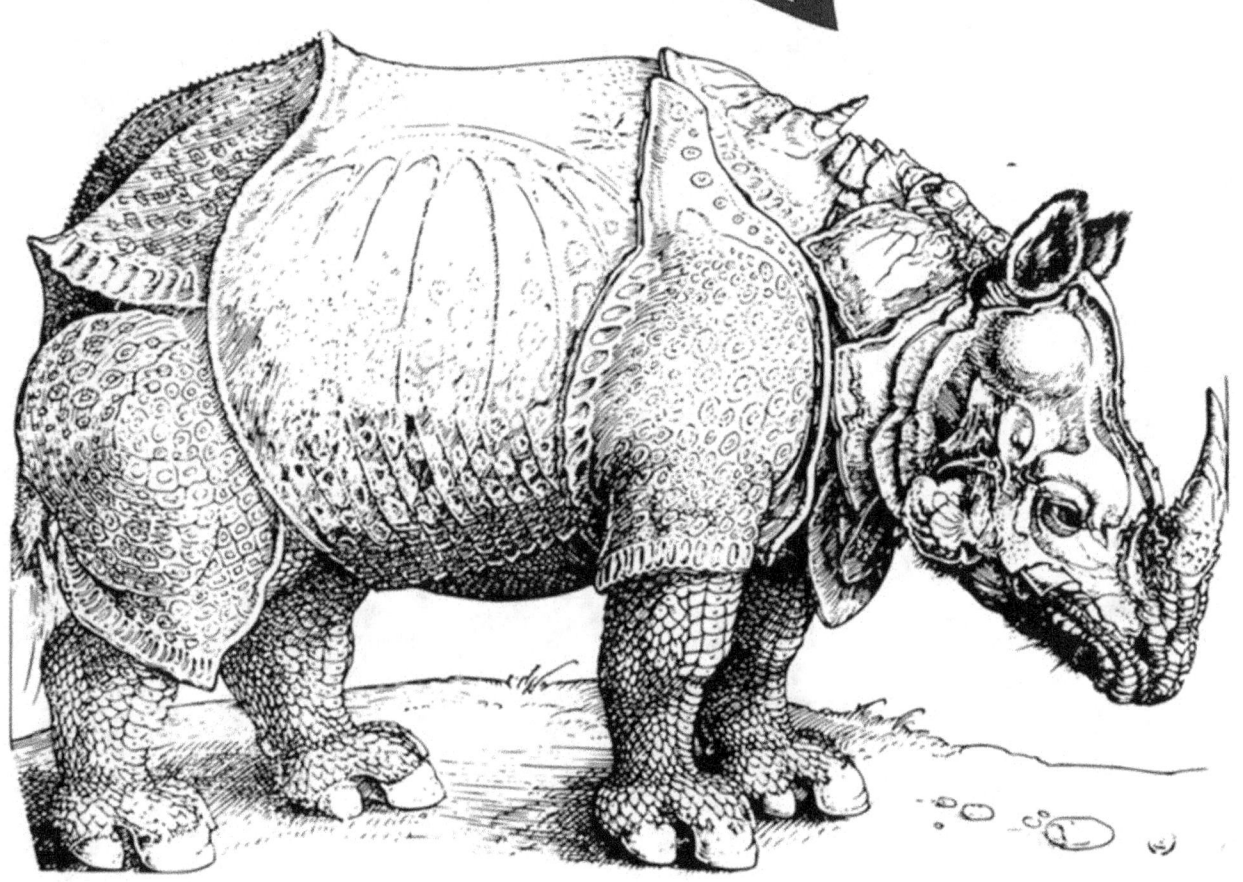

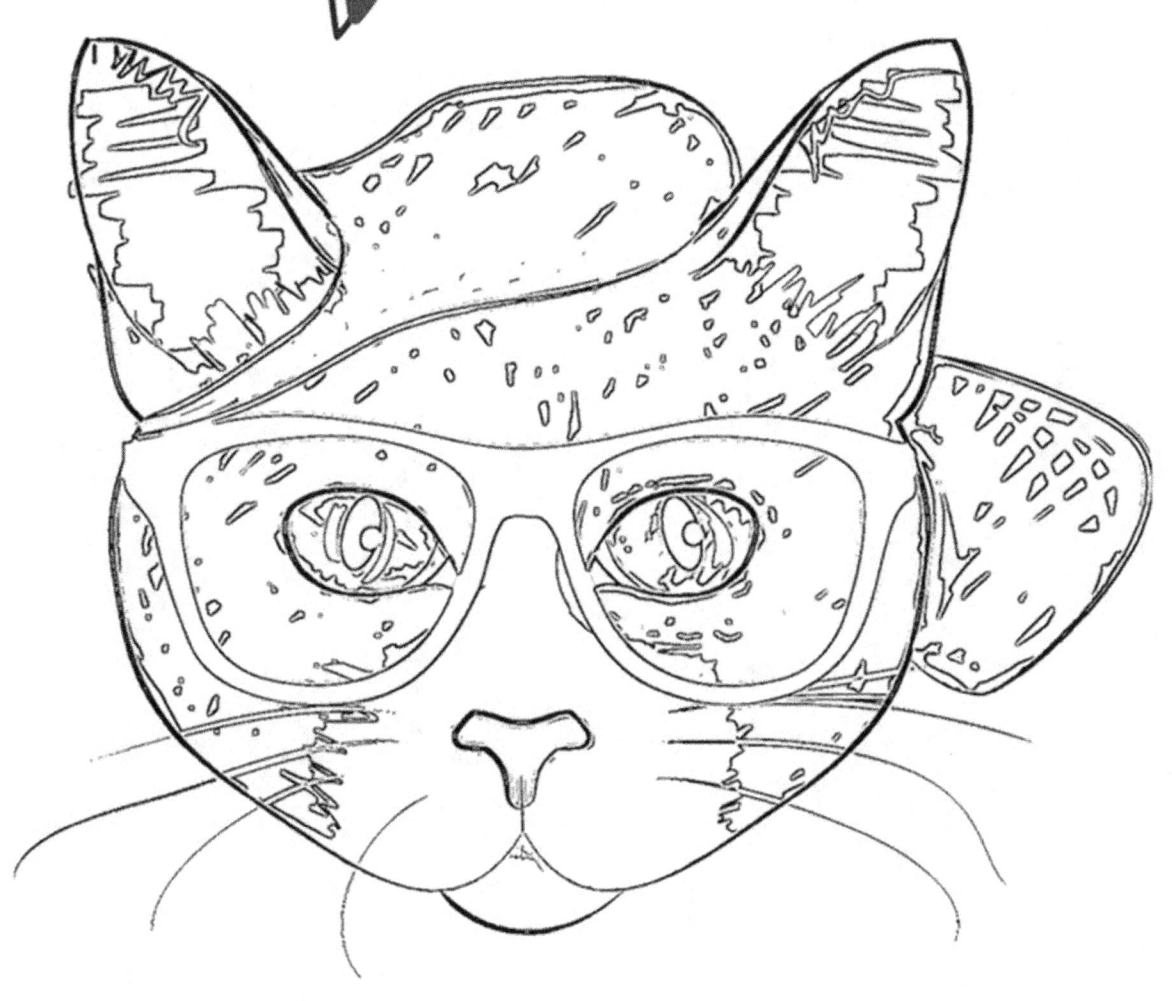

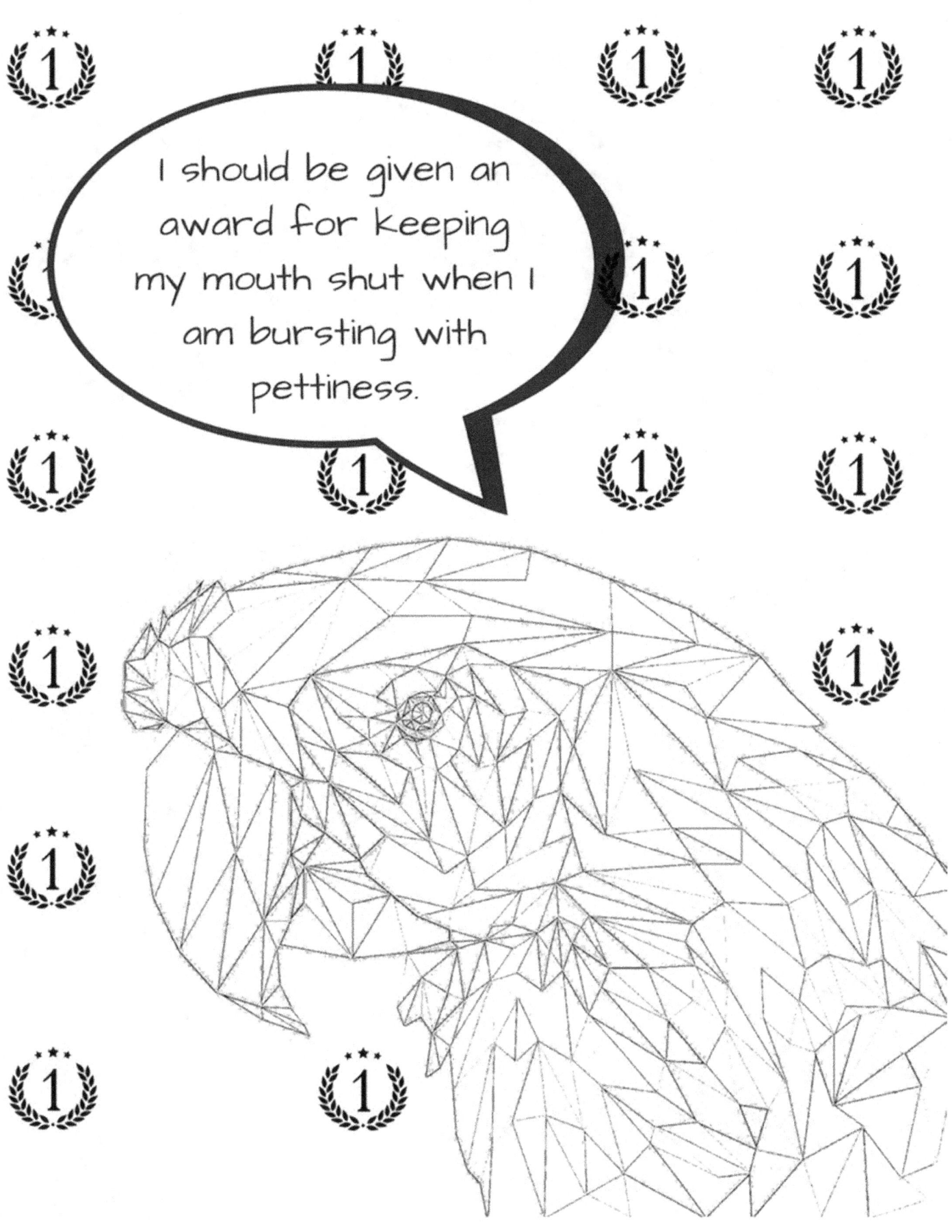

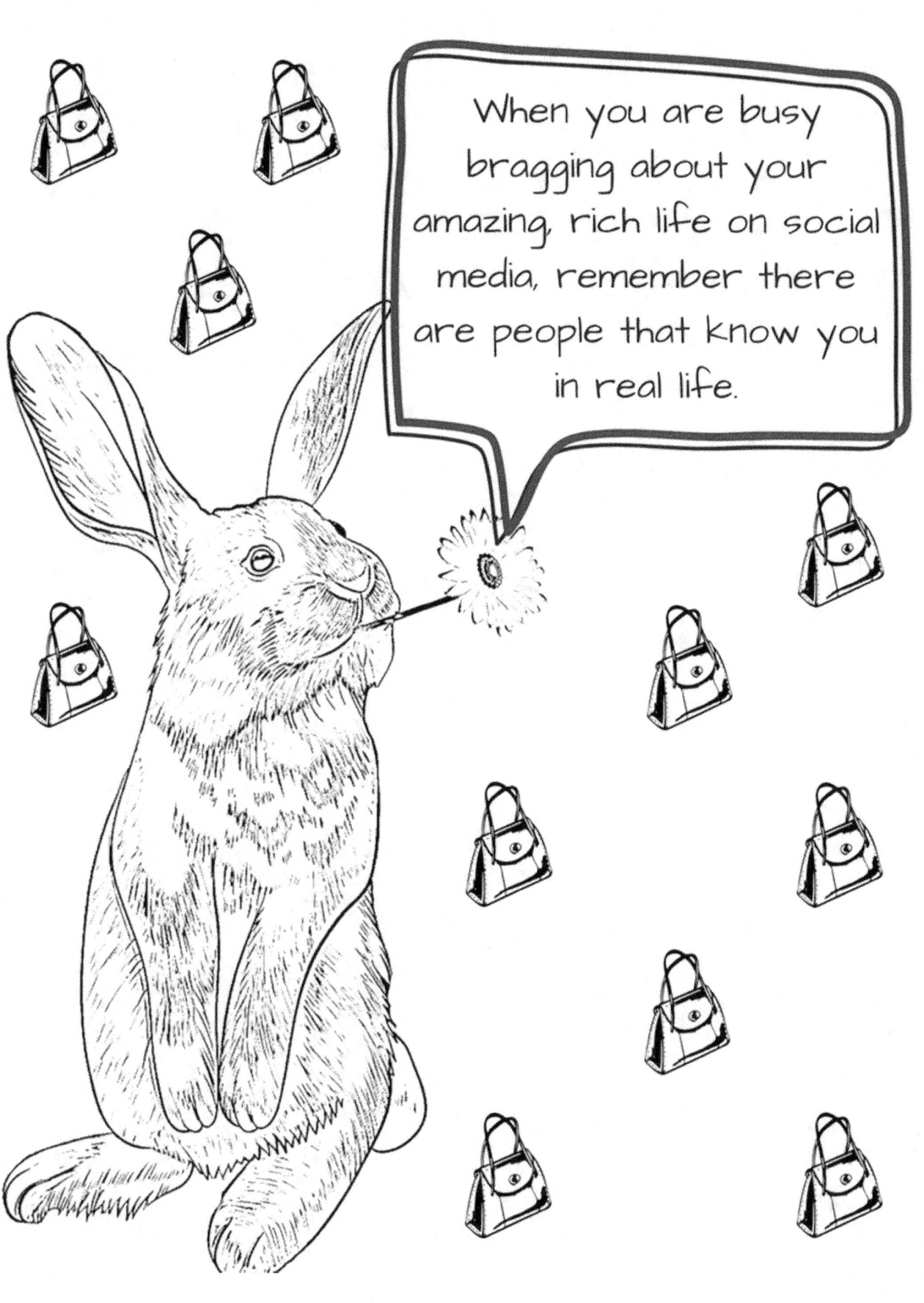

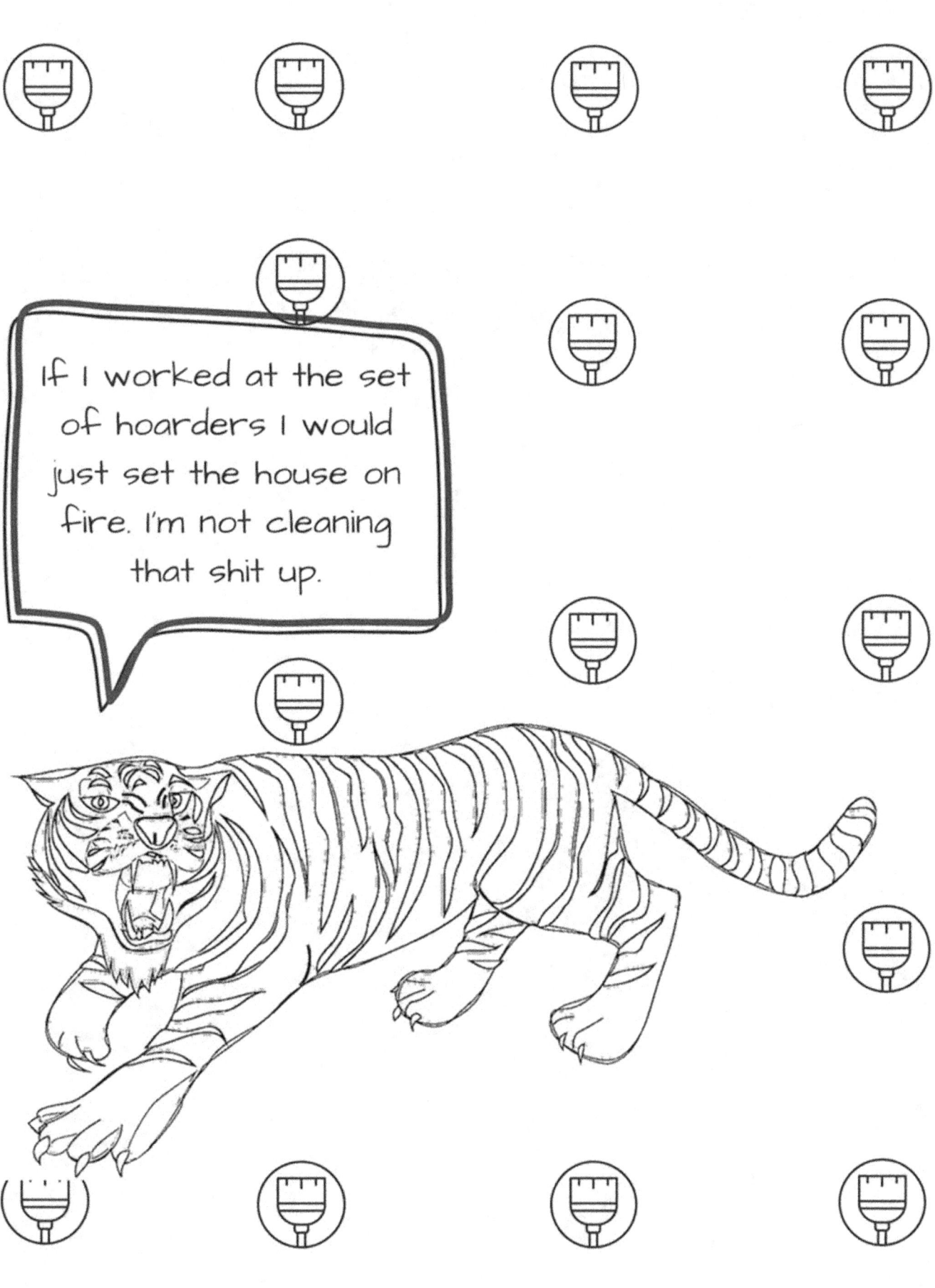

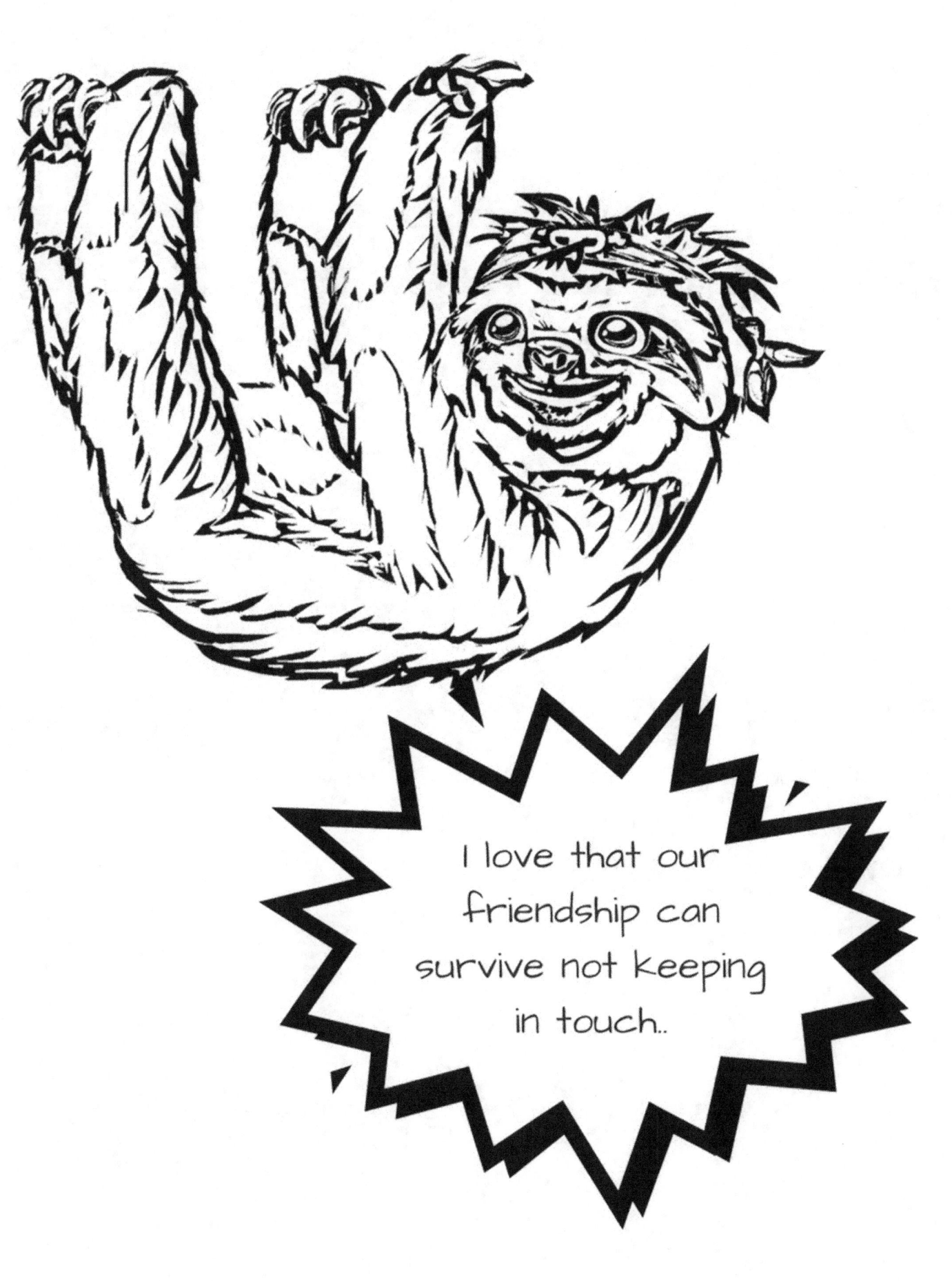

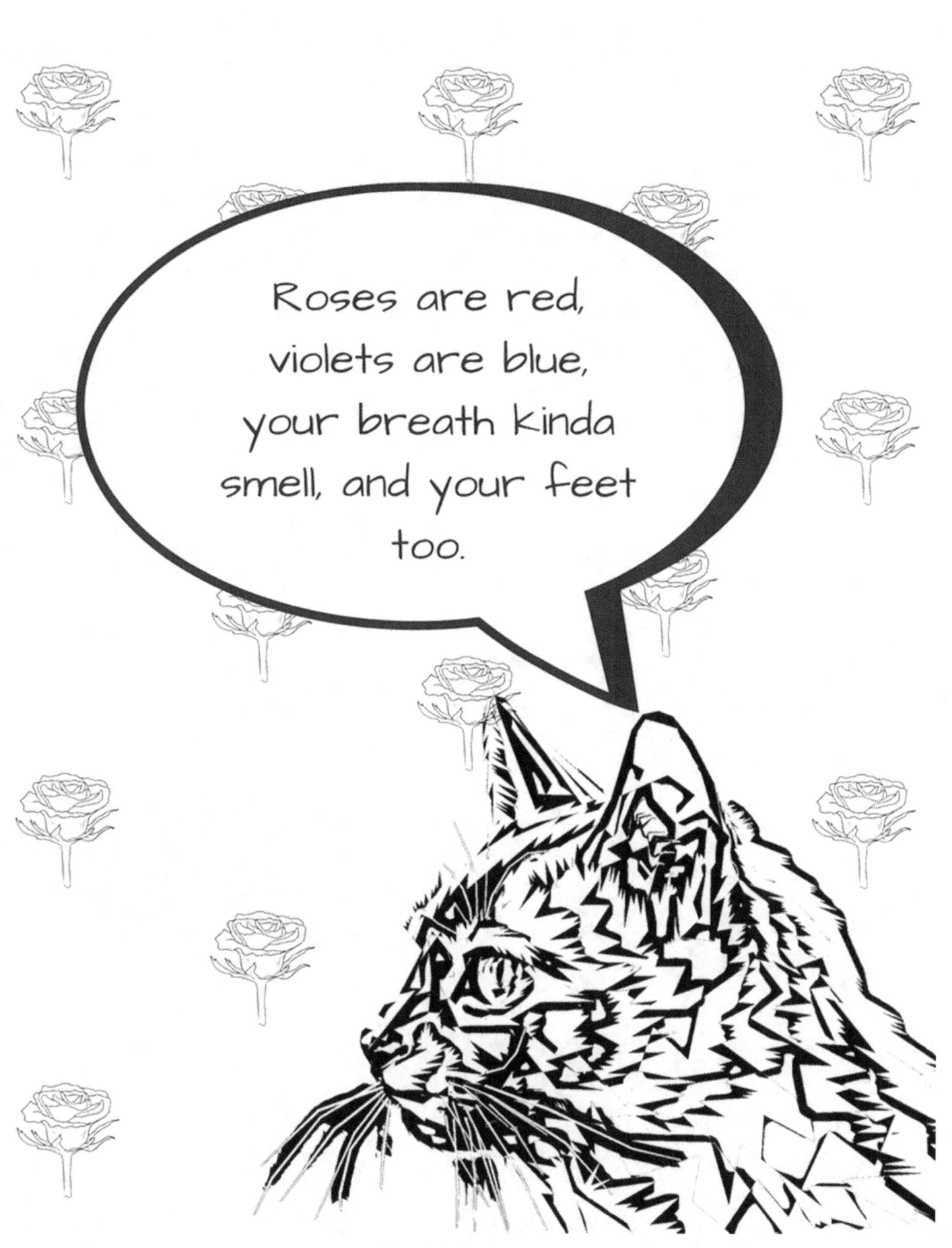

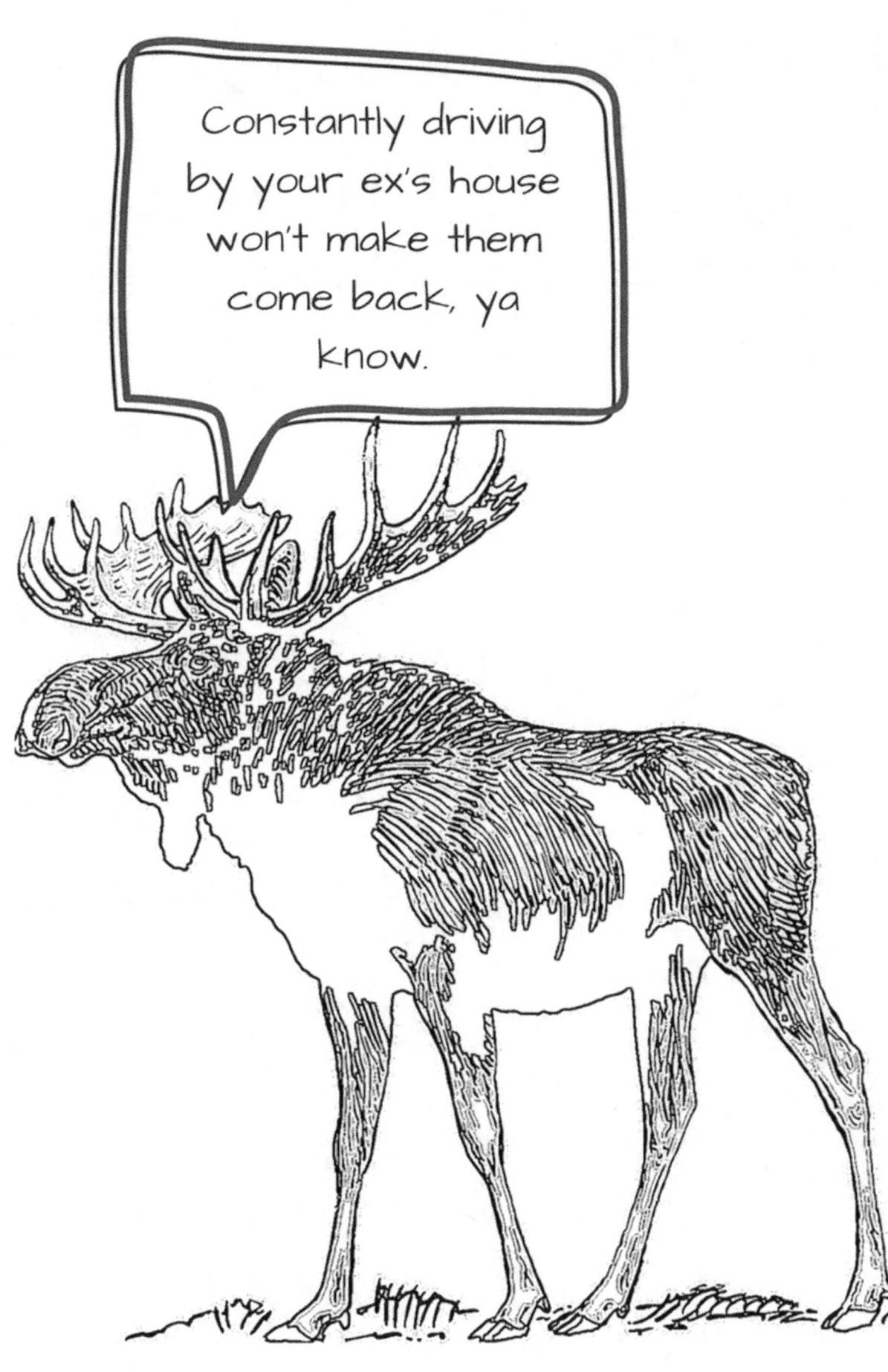

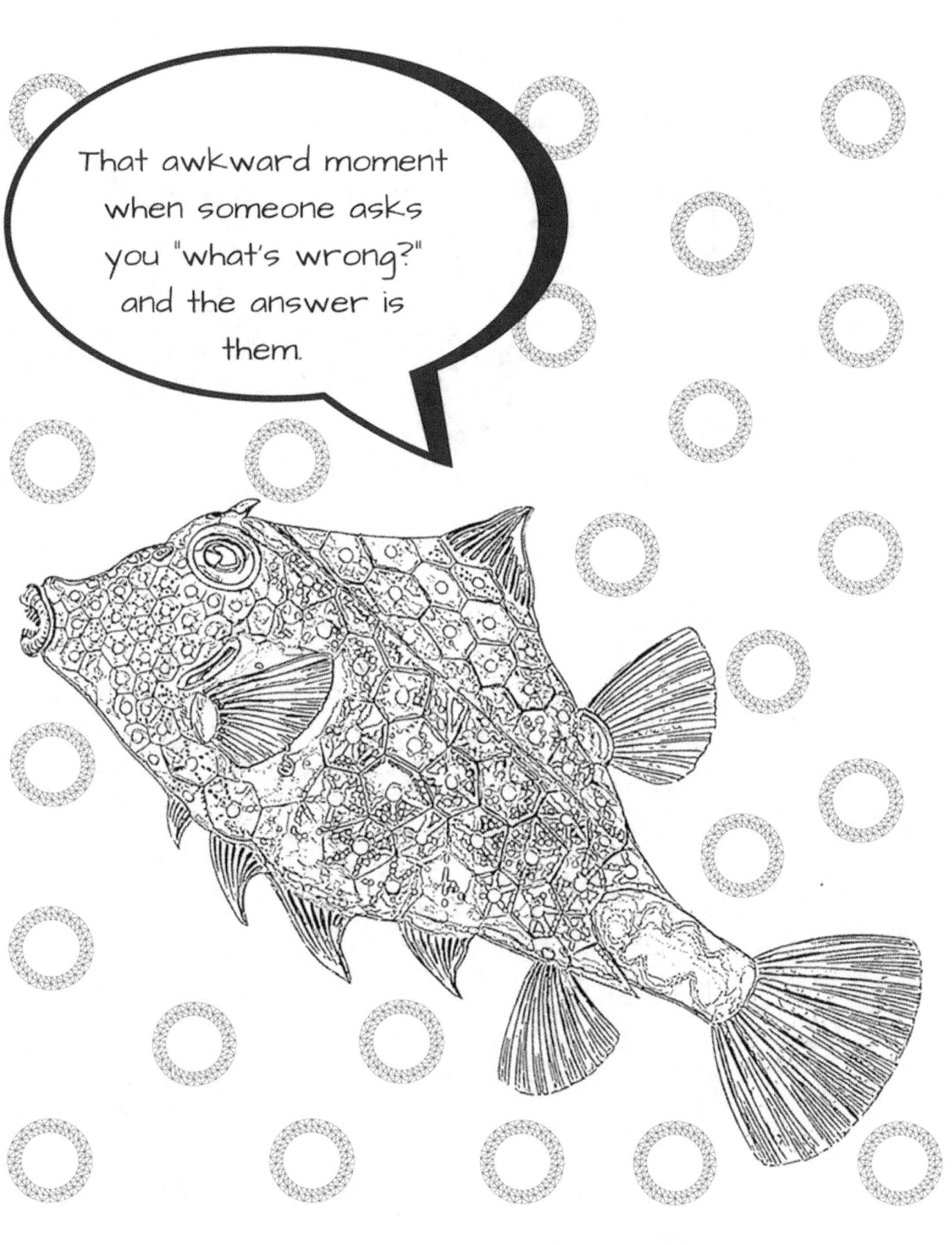

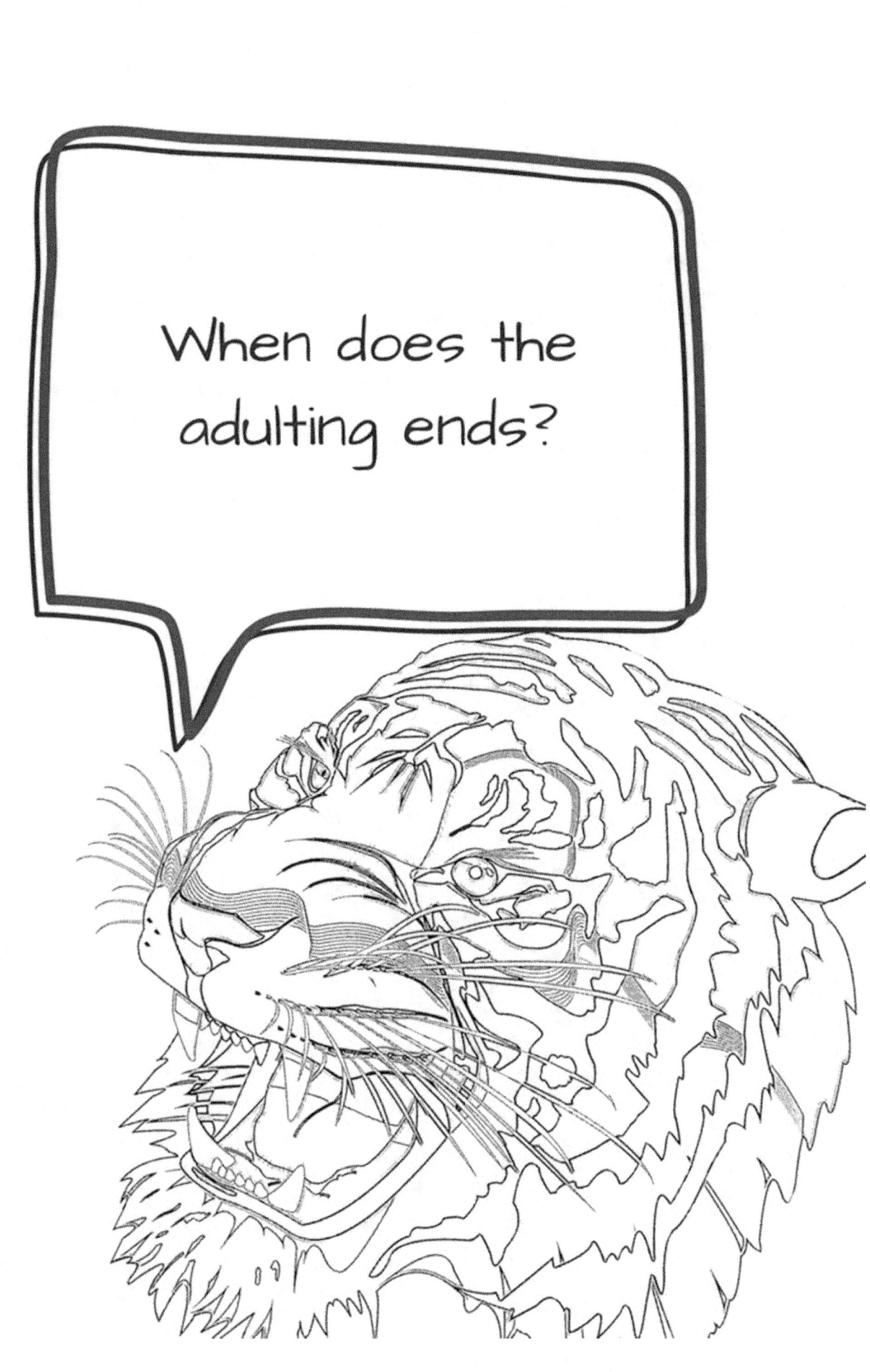

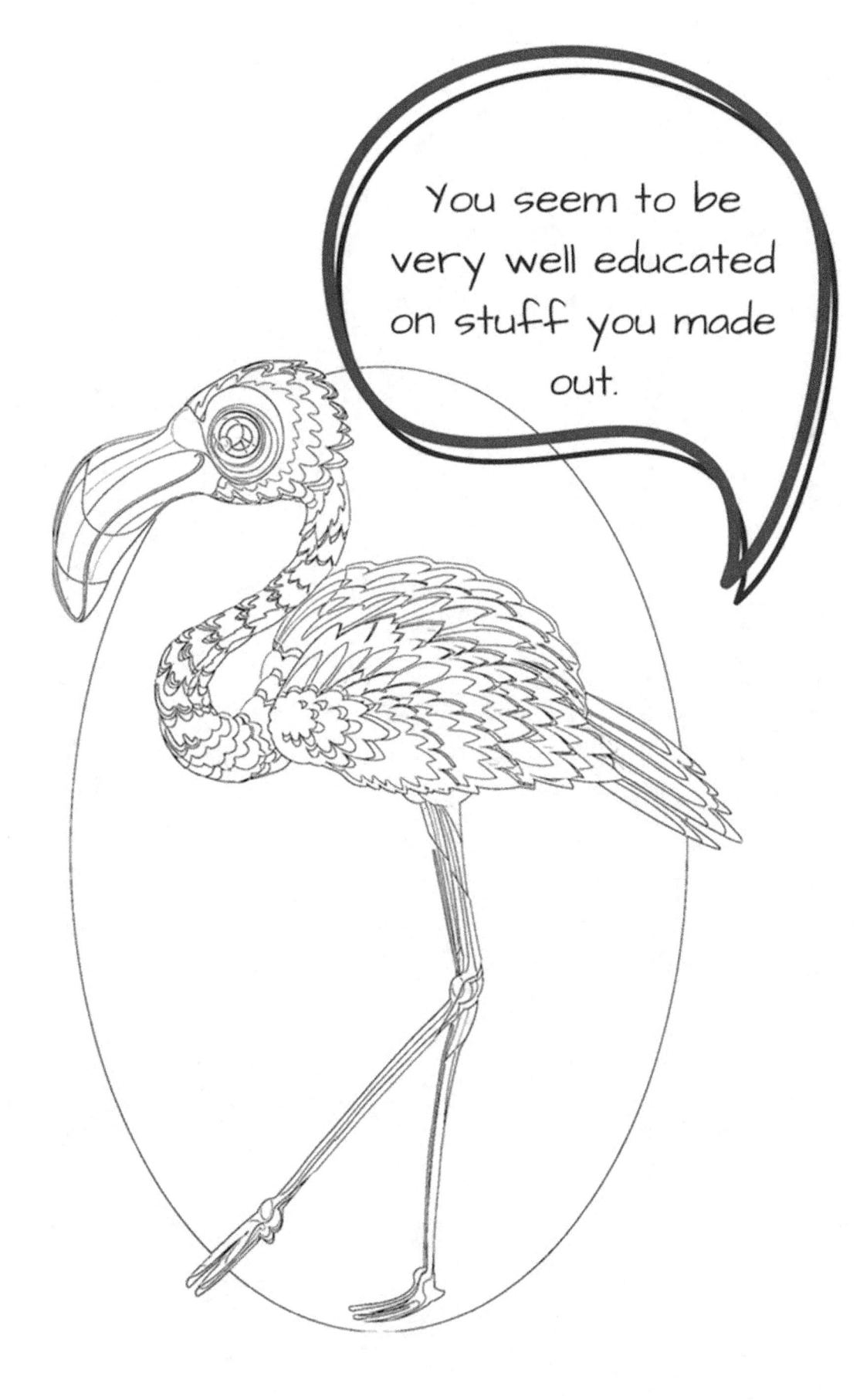

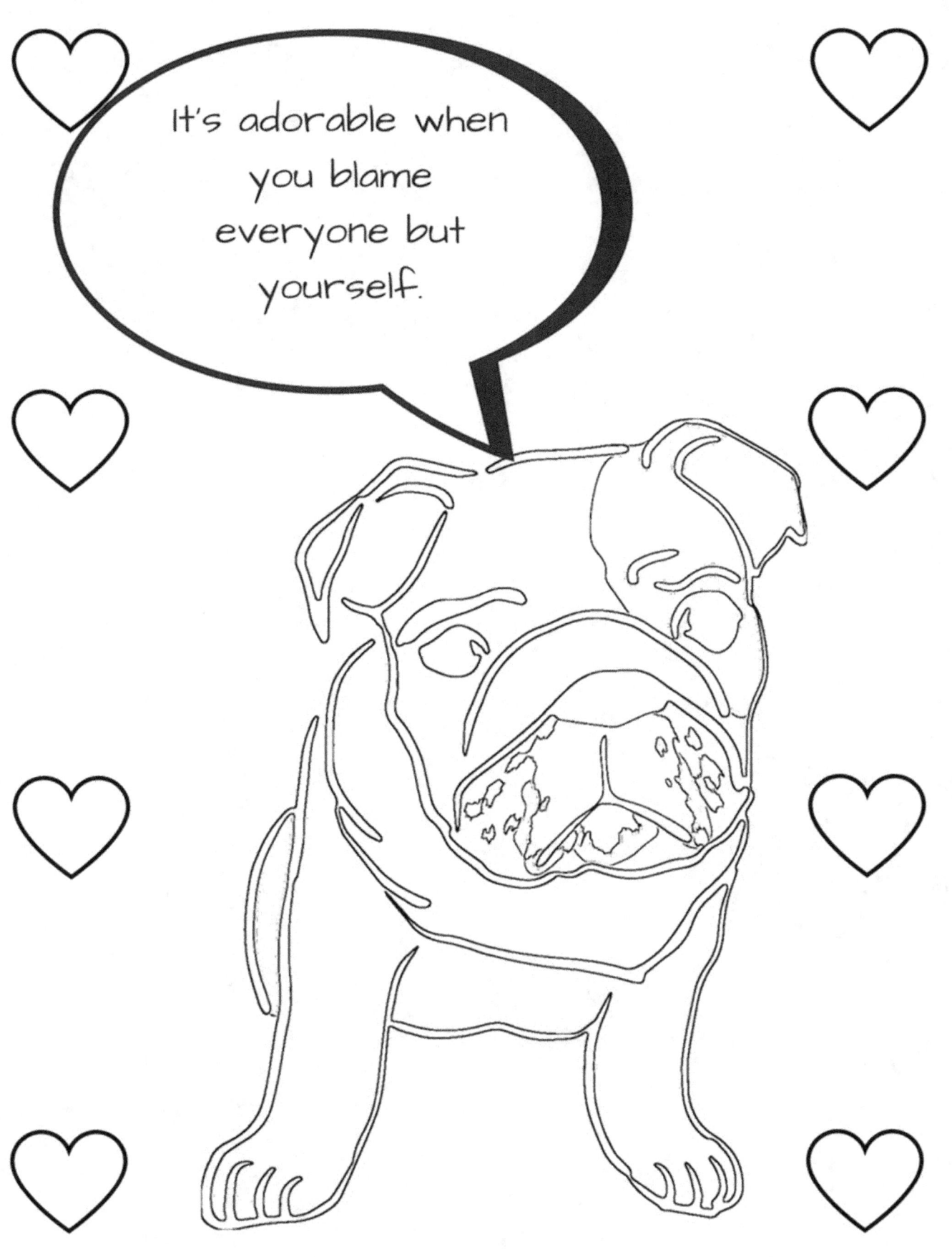

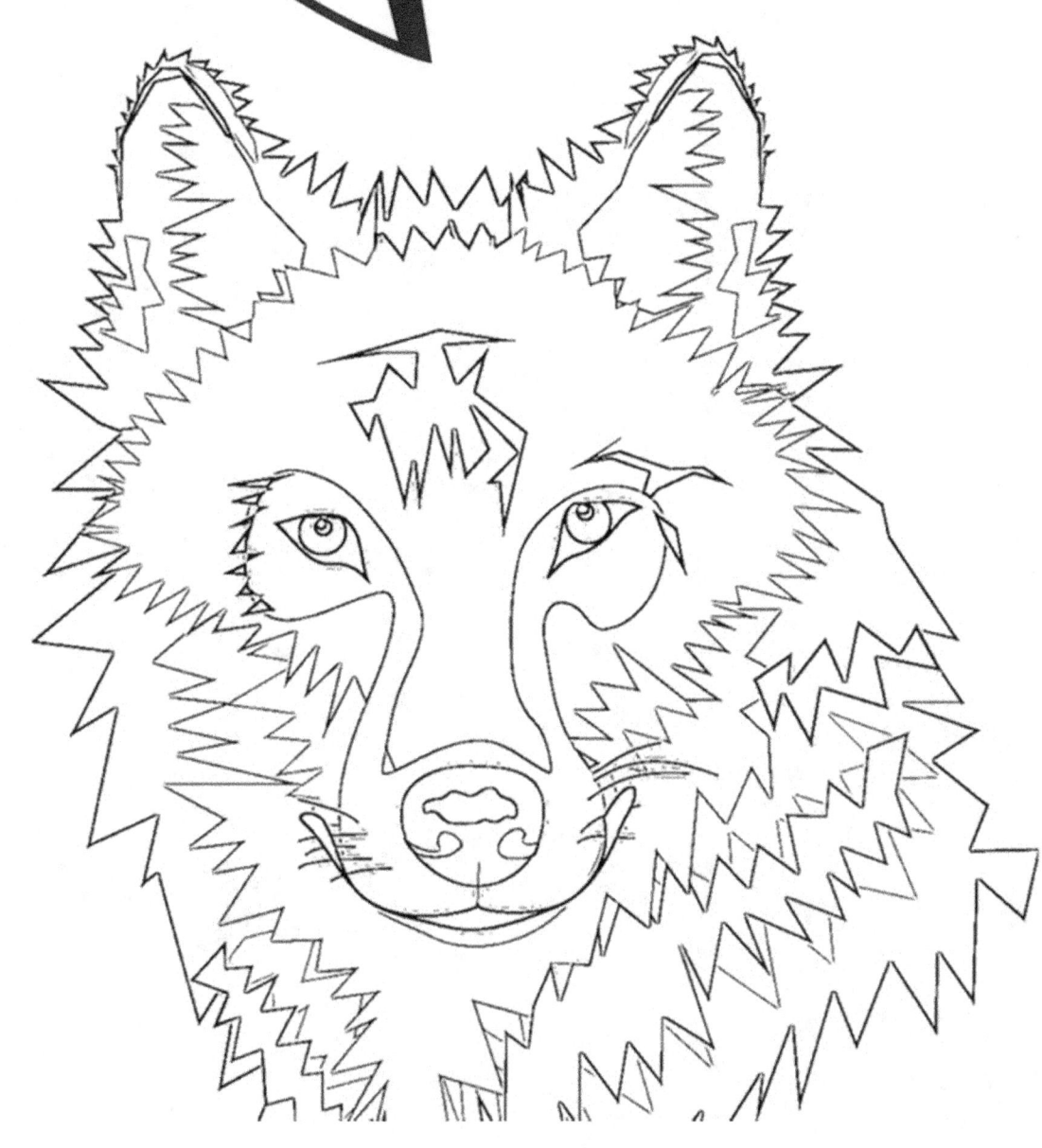

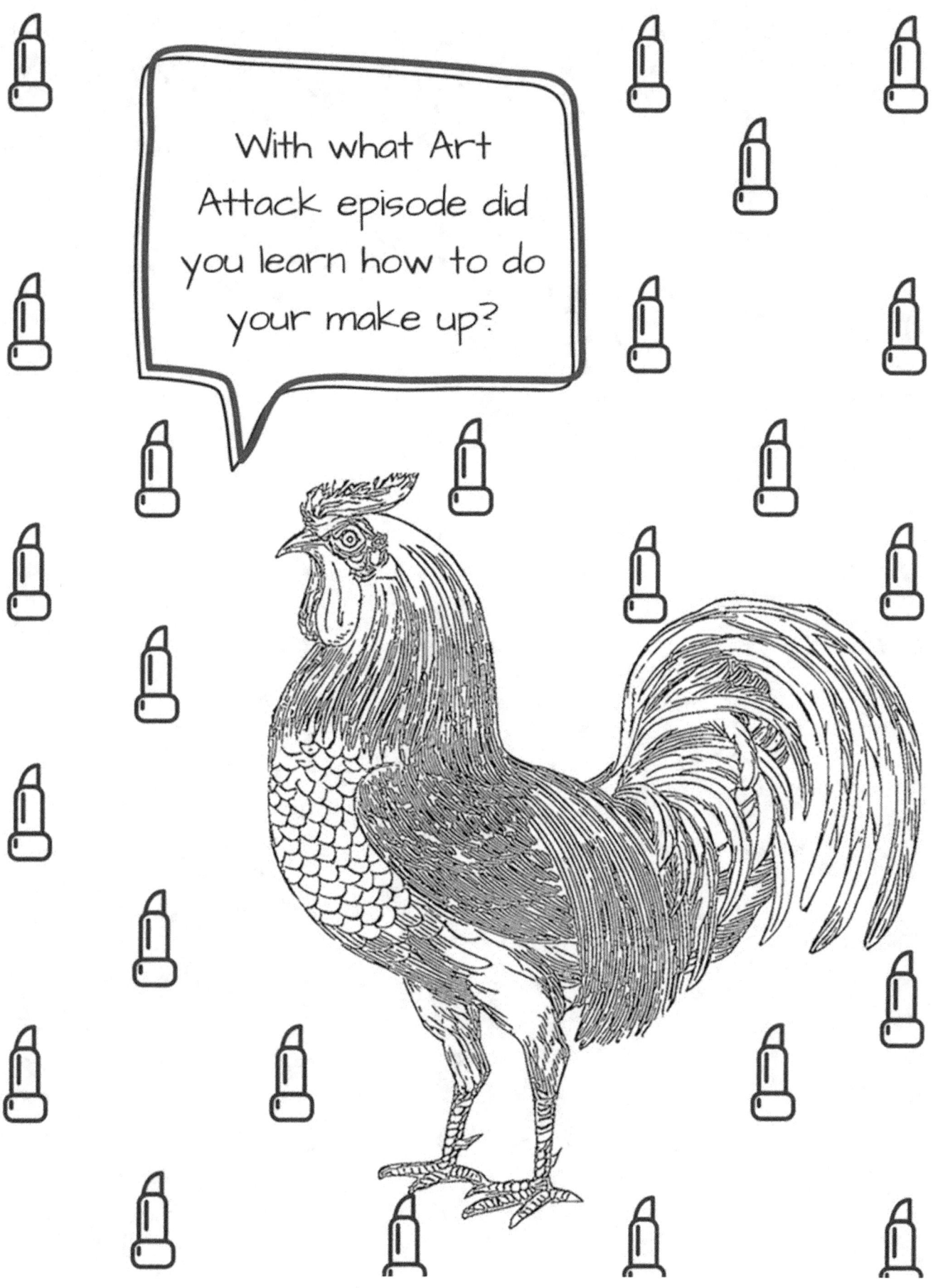

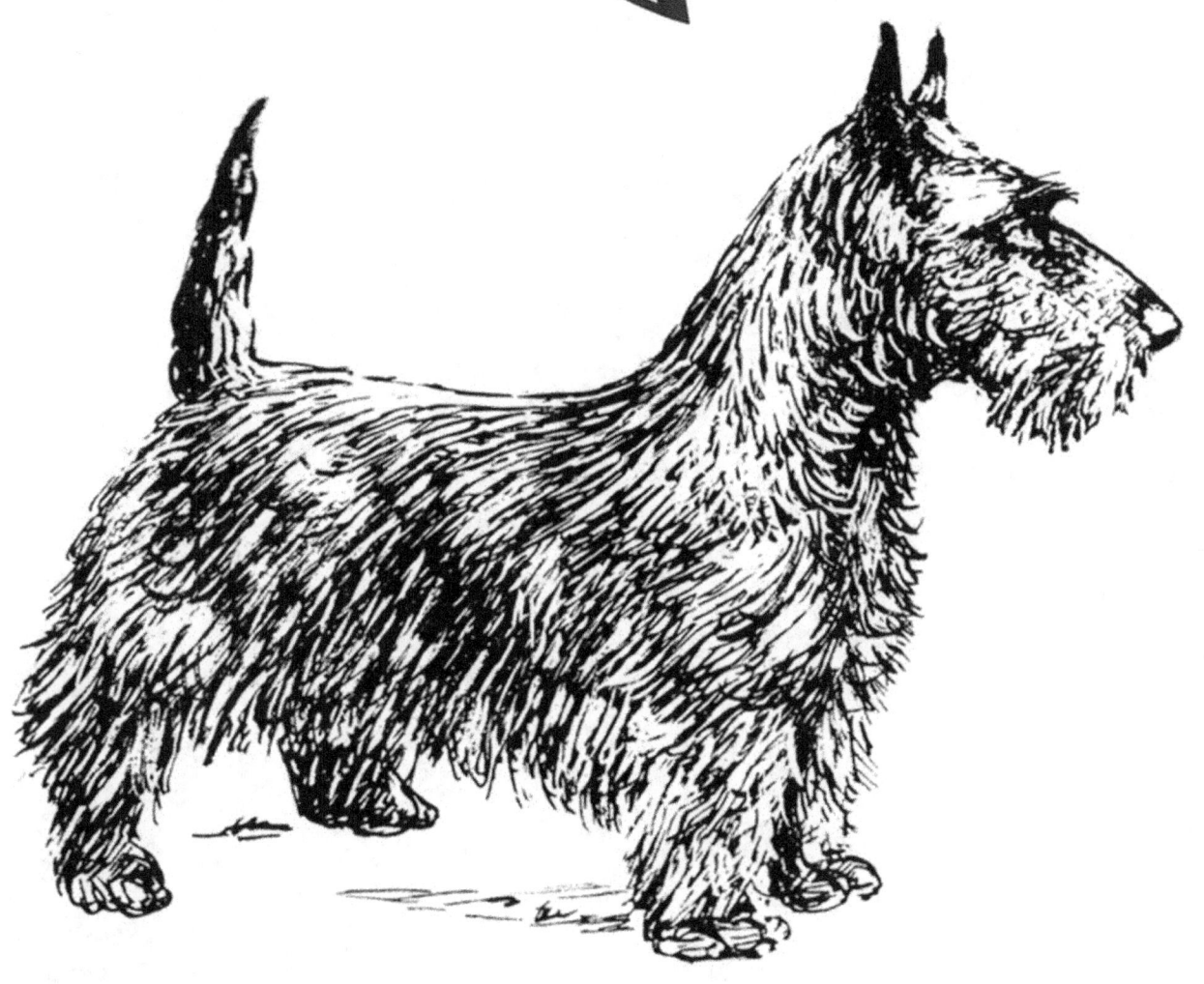

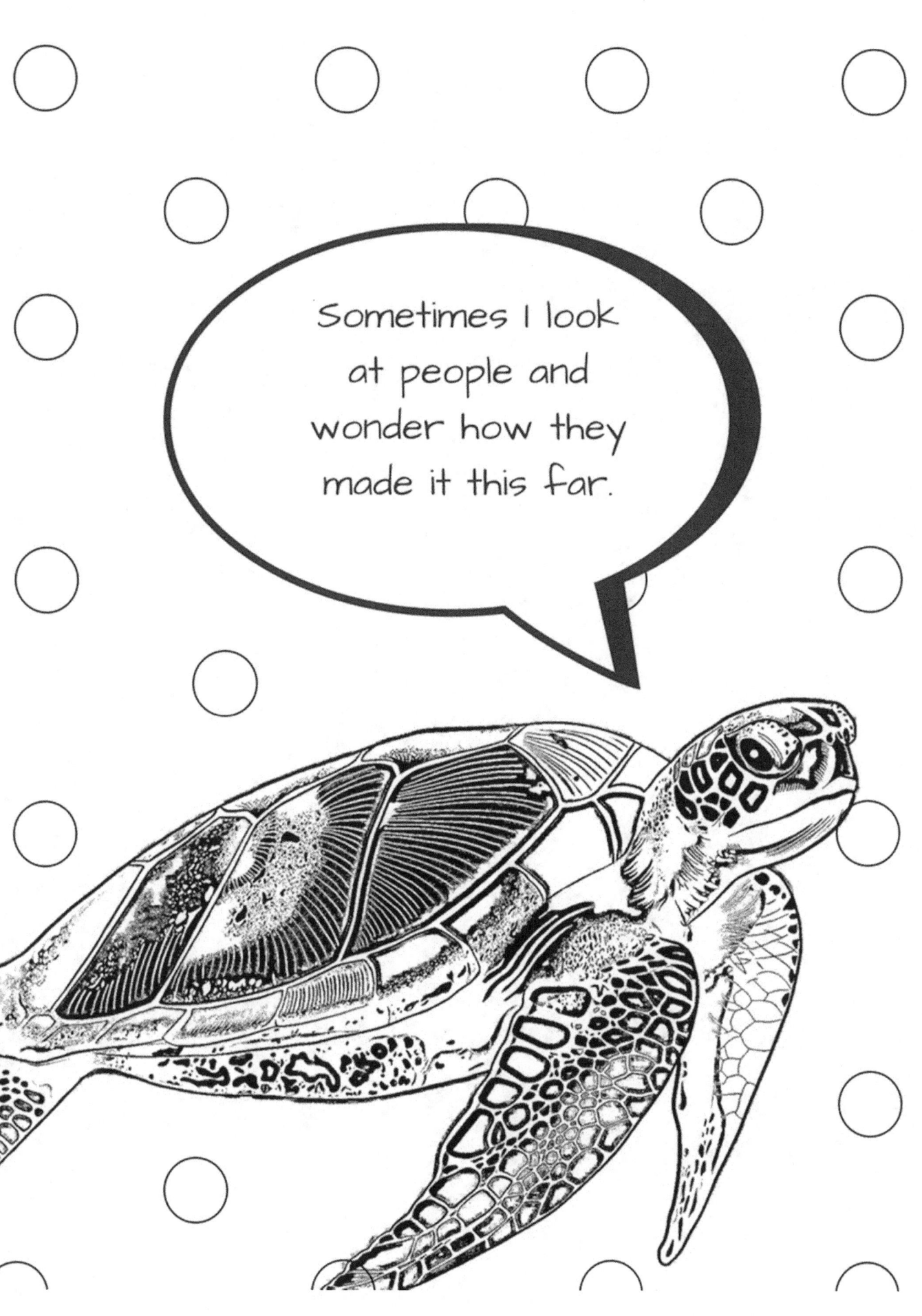

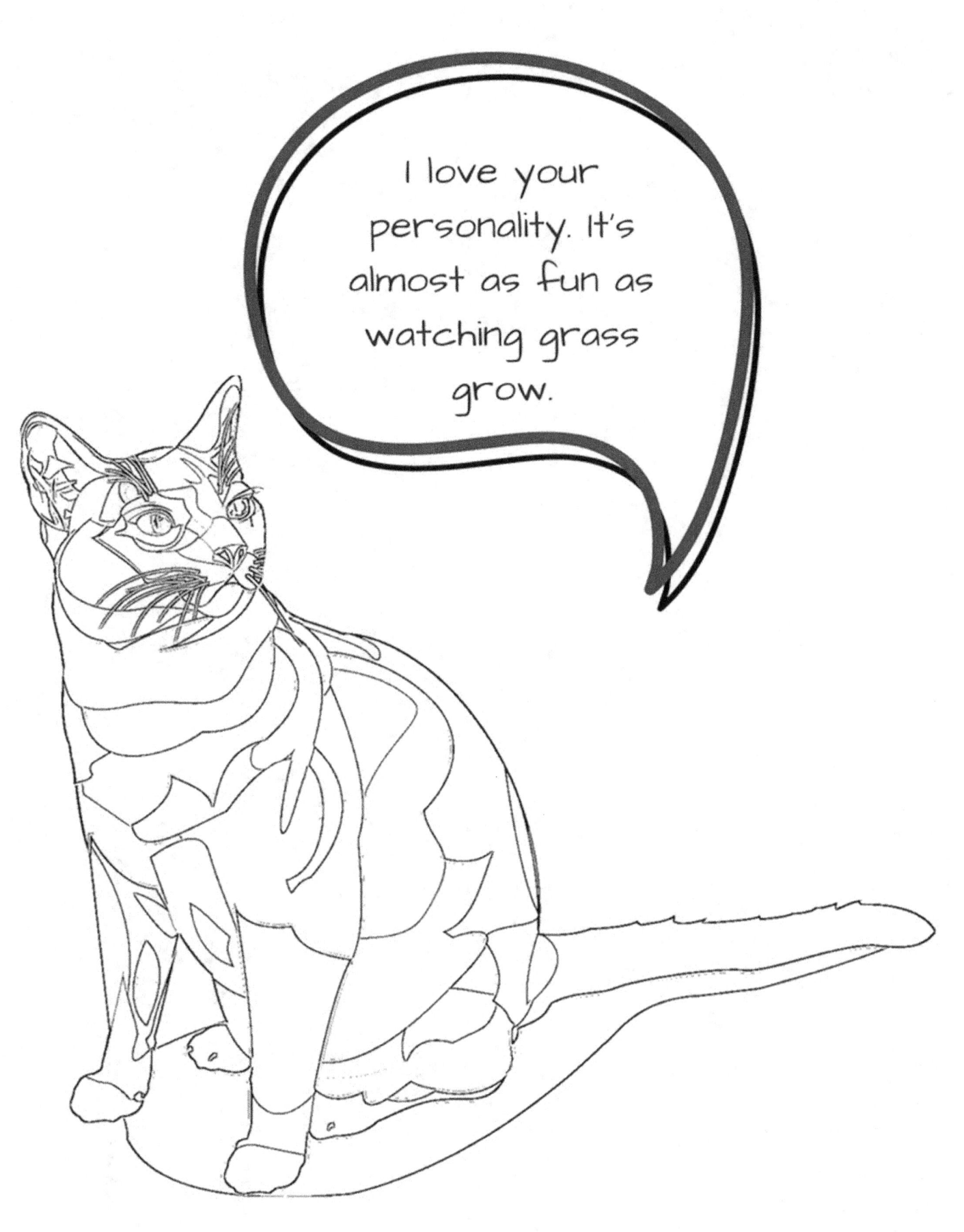

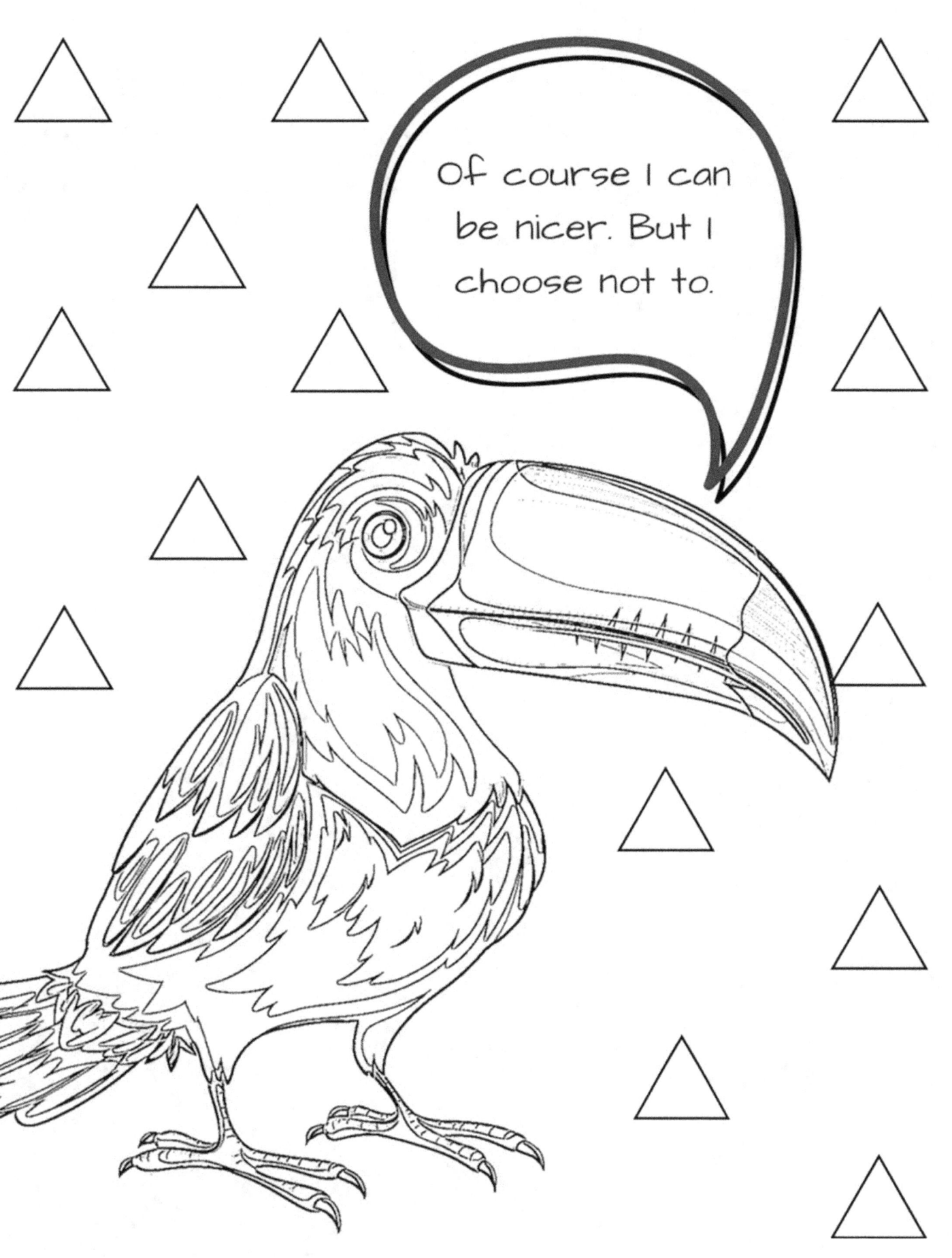

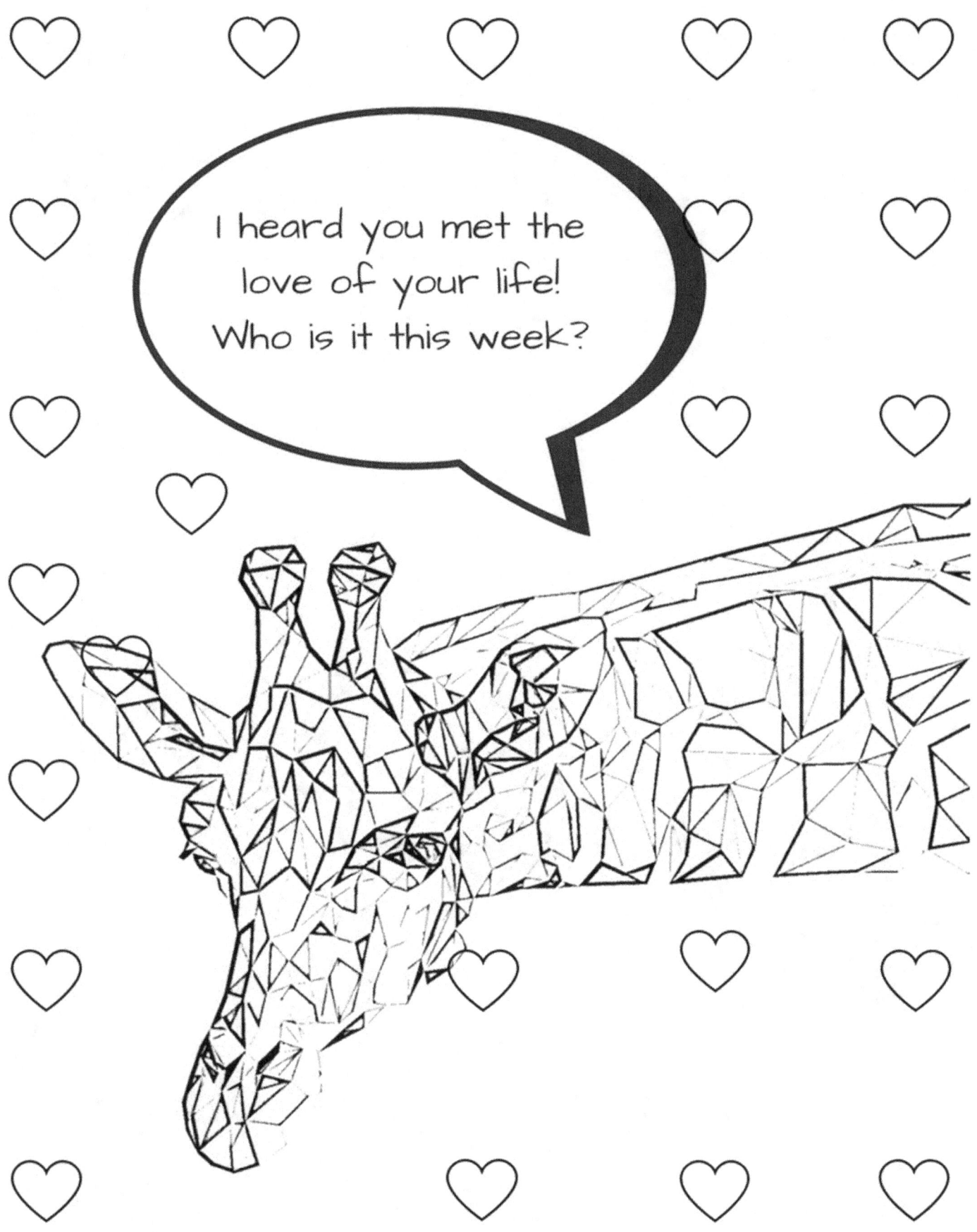

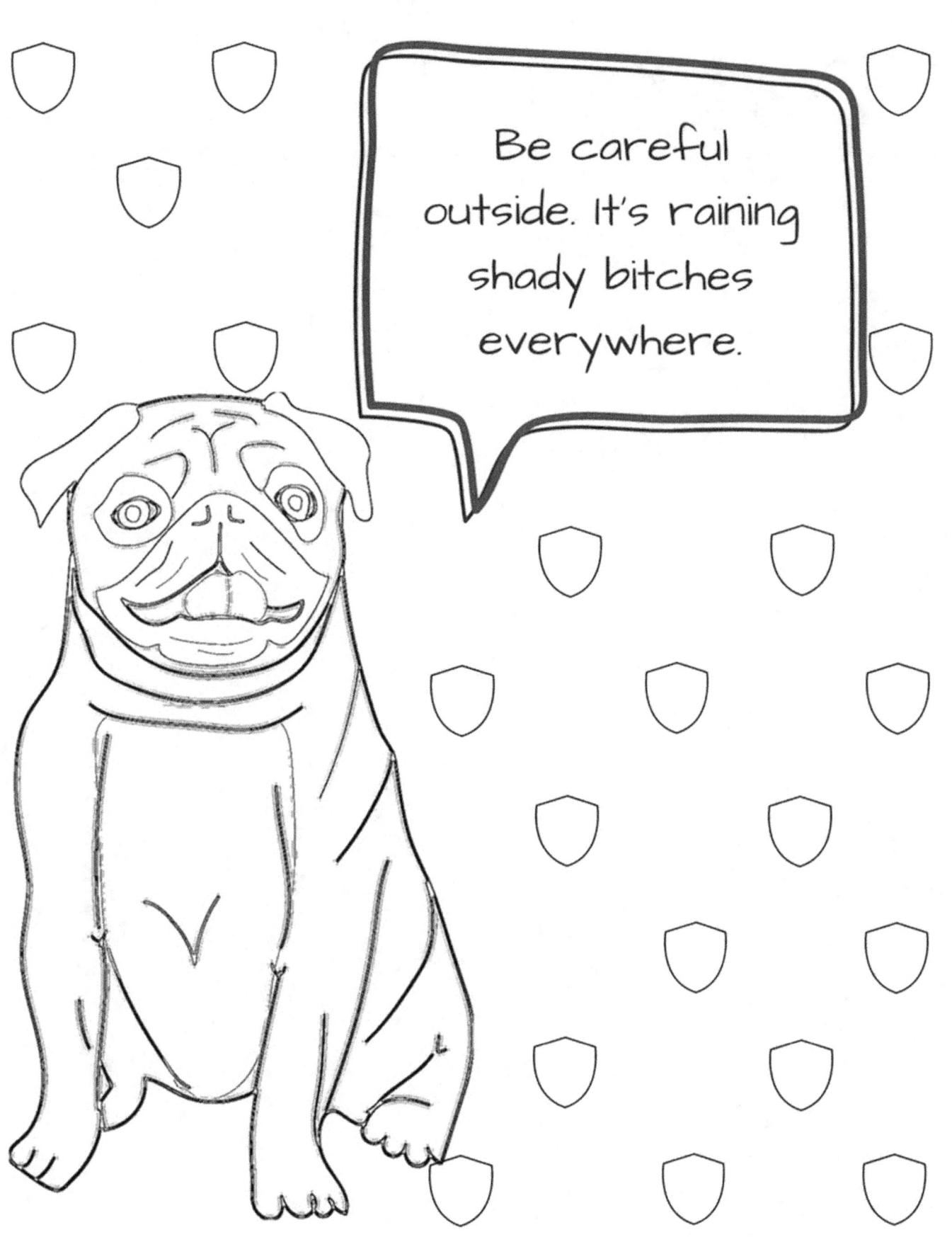

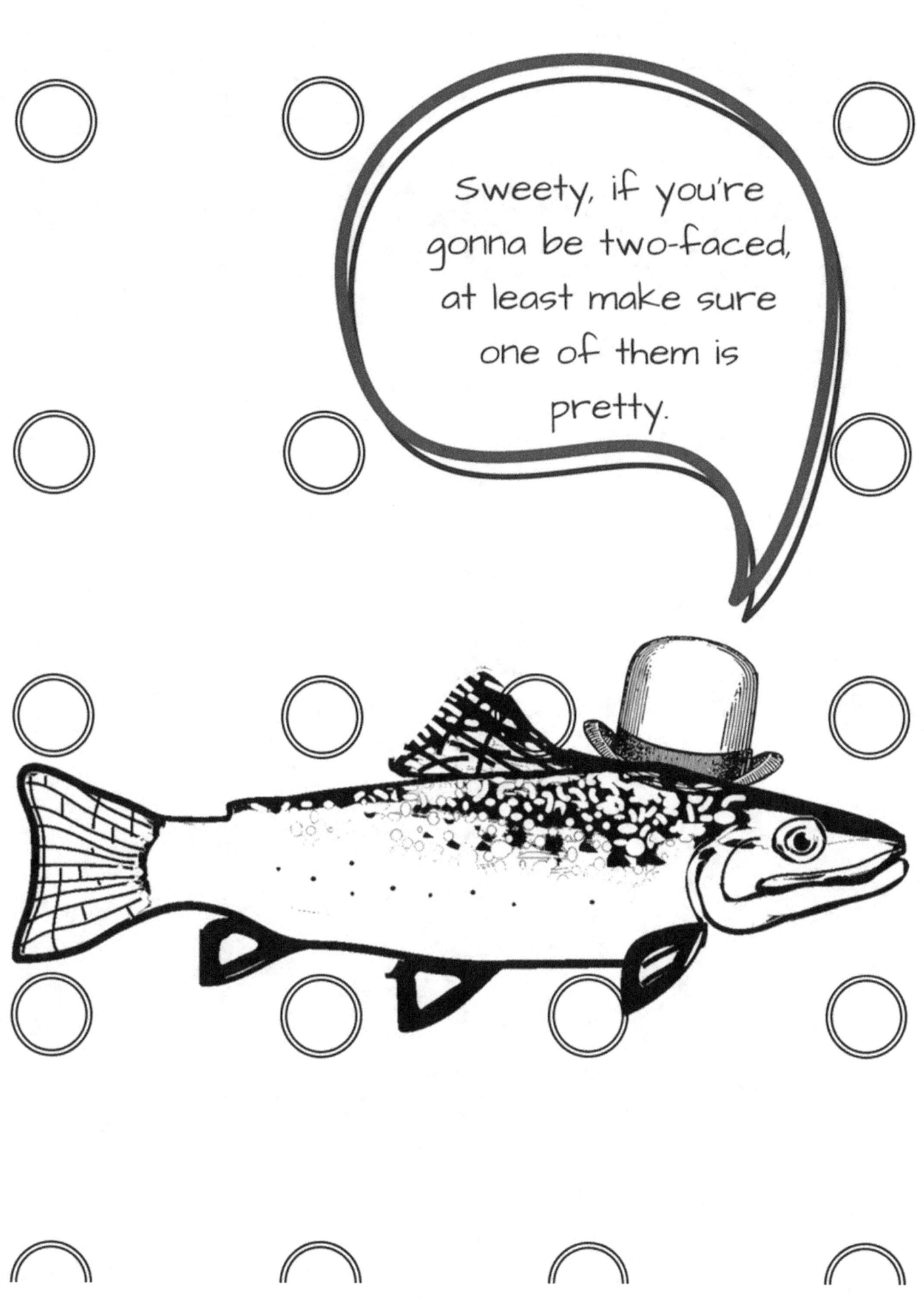

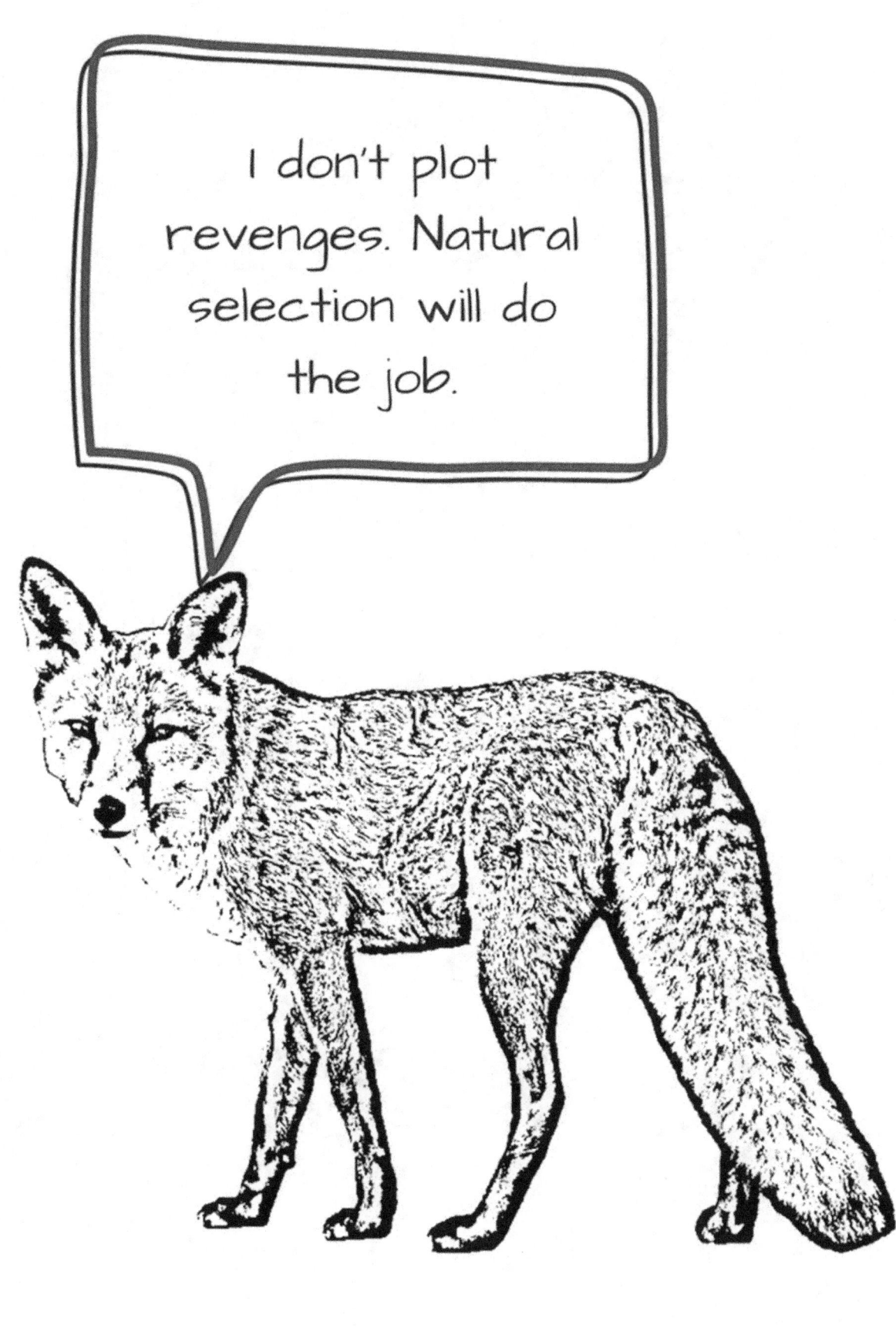

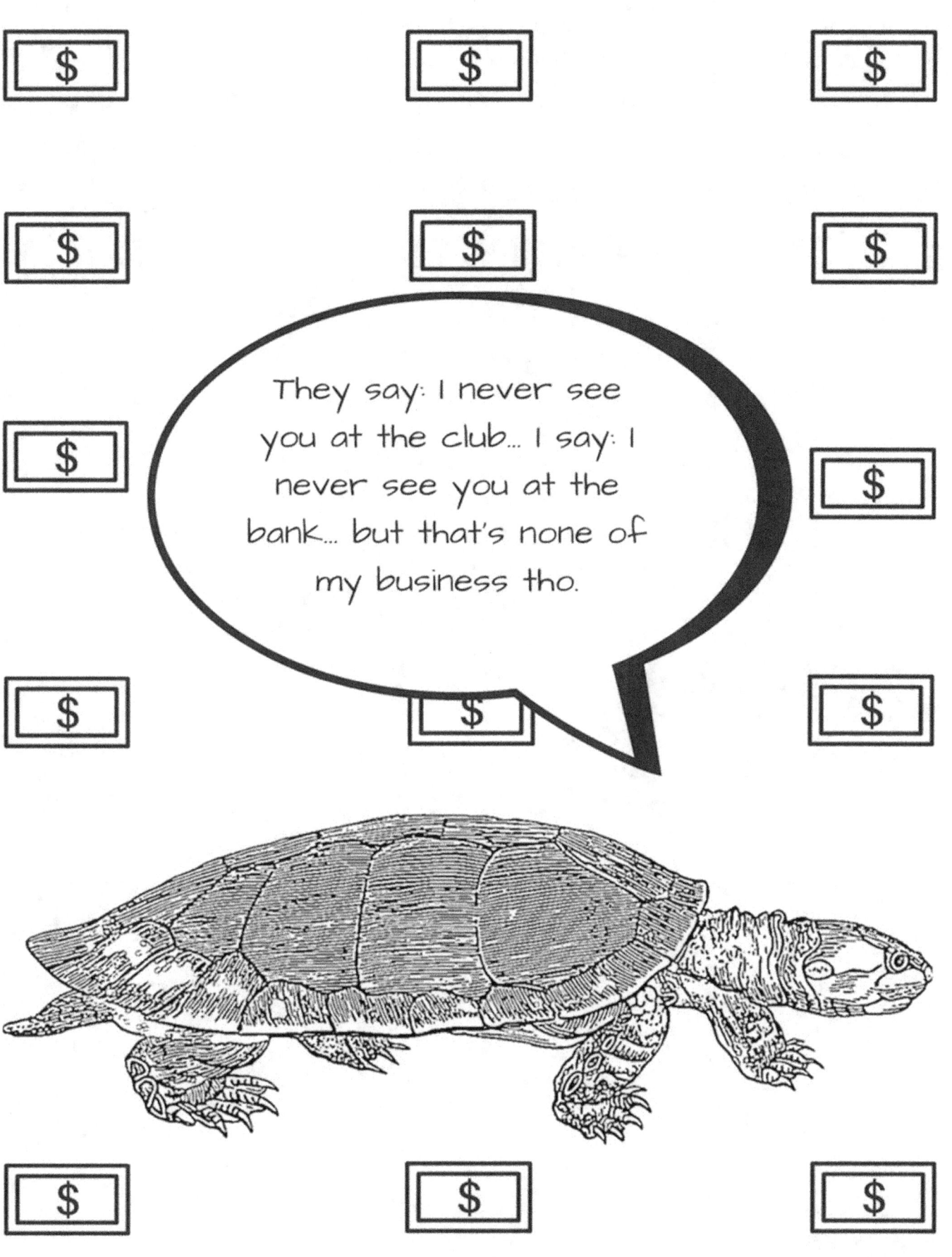

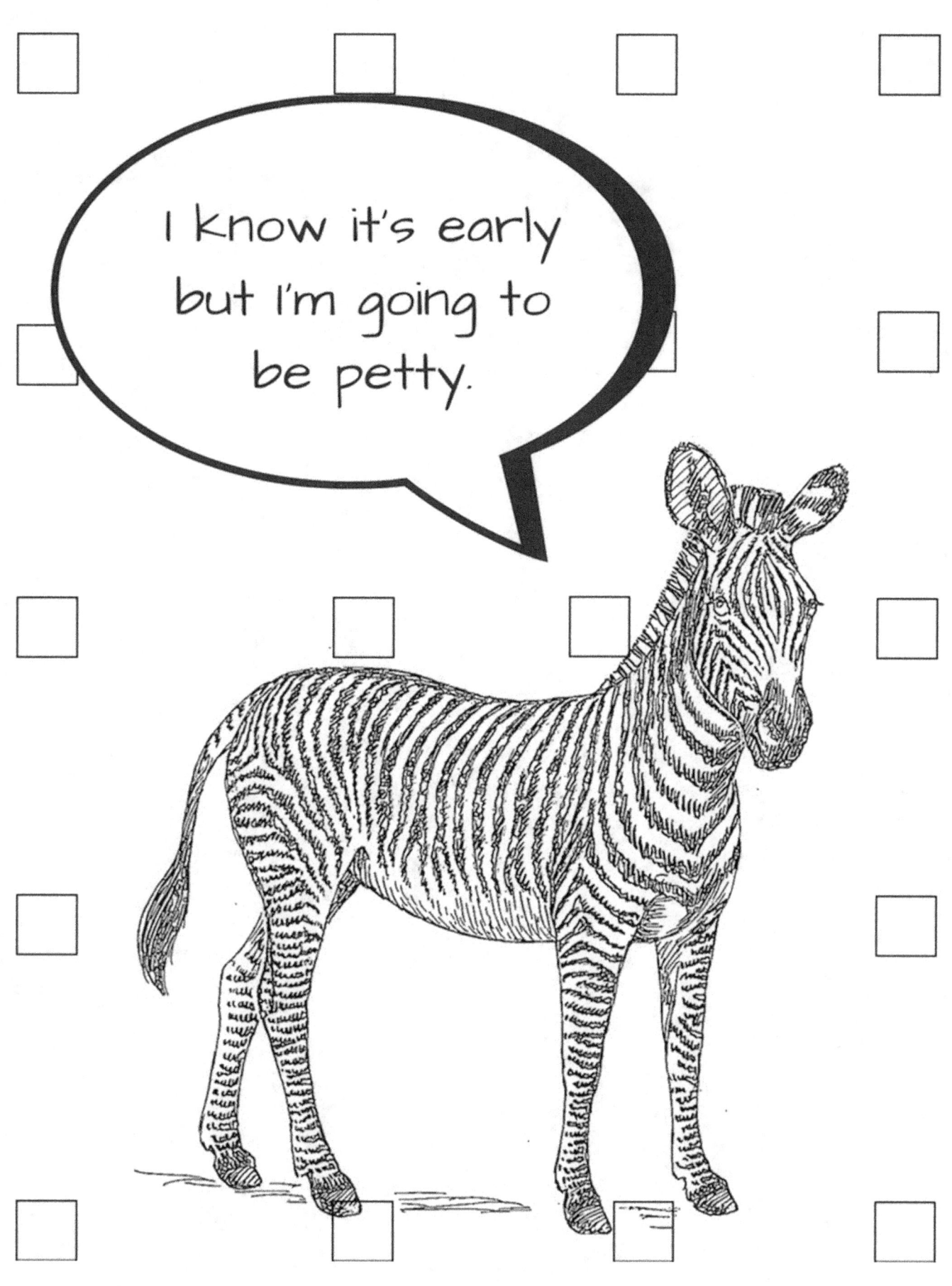

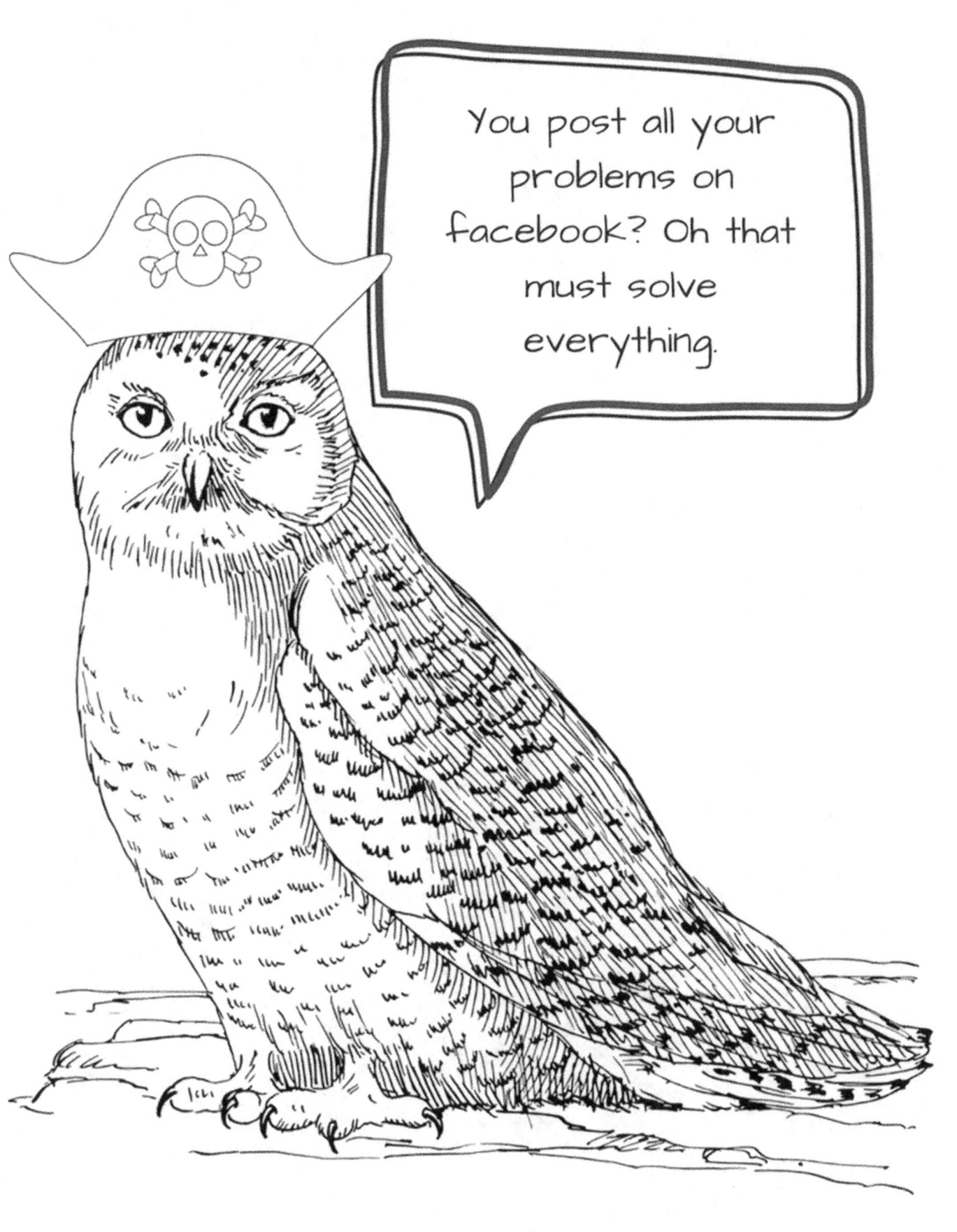

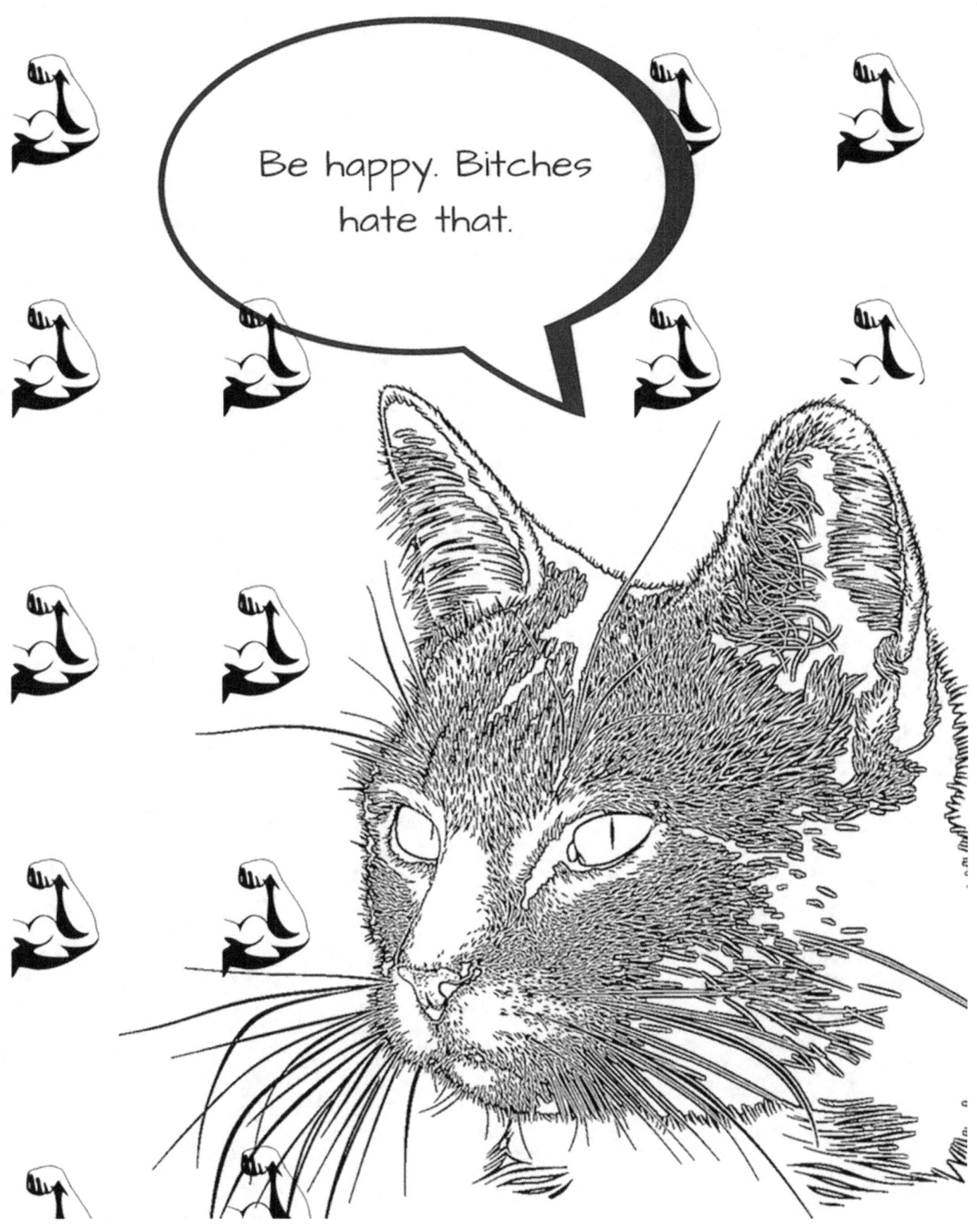